Cécile Catherine

Wonderful Paris

Translated by Angela Moyon

ÉDITIONS OUEST-FRANCE
13 rue du Breil, Rennes

Café de Flore (top).

Booksellers on the banks of the Seine.

In the Père-Lachaise Cemetery (bottom).

The Eiffel Tower at dusk (front cover).

The Louvre pyramid (back cover).

The Pont des Arts and the Ile de la Cîté.

INTRODUCTION

From the first traces of human habitation during Prehistoric times up to the gigantic local authority that we see today, the destiny of Paris has created the history and the past of France itself.

Its main attraction was geographical in nature—the Seine drew the Celts of the Parisii tribe to the Ile de la Cité, the marshland which became known as Lutetia. Led by Julius Caesar, the Roman invaders who gained overall mastery of the country in 52 B.C. extended their sovereignty to the Left Bank. They occupied the town for more than three centuries, bringing it « Pax romana » and its very first commercial activities within a civilisation which has left us remains such as the Arena of Lutetia or the baths in the Cluny Residence. With the arrival of the Barbarians in the latter part of the 3rd Century, peace was shattered and the Roman emperors Julian and Valentinian, who lived in the first palace on the island (the forerunner of the Law Courts), strengthened their hold on authority. The population again huddled close to the walled Ile de la Cité. In 508, Clovis defeated the Huns and established Merovingian supremacy on the island, which had taken the name « Paris. » Pippin the Short became the first of the Carolingian monarchs in 751; with the coming of Charlemagne, the lineage was to favour Germany and Aix-la-Chapelle to the detriment of Paris which suffered

The Fountain of Innocents.

invasion from the Vikings in the 9th century. In 987, when the first king in the third dynasty, Hugh Capet, mounted the throne, Paris was firmly established as the capital from which power was to radiate throughout the entire area of what we now know as the Paris Basin. The town's importance was soon to cause problems with provincial nobility. Paris, though, developed its own structure and began to prosper, thanks mainly to the advantages of the river. This was the time chosen by Bishop Maurice de Sully to build one of the finest

examples of Parisian architecture — Notre-Dame. In the 12th century, Philip Augustus fixed the boundaries of the capital within a new wall which was quickly to prove too restricting. At the same time, the creation of the university and numerous colleges was accompanied by an increase in the population and the urbanisation of the town which acquired a council in 1260 headed by the Dean of Guilds. The Right Bank, too, became inhabited with the setting up of the first market. On the foreign affairs front the English, who had set

their hearts on the kingdom of France, began the One Hundred Years' War in 1337. This was the indirect cause of the death of the Dean of Guilds, Etienne Marcel, who rebelled against royal authority in 1357. Peace returned for a short time during the reign of Charles V who had the Bastille Prison built and the Louvre extended. The 15th century was marked by the bloody return of the war with Joan of Arc's moment of devotion to duty and the consecration of King Henry VI of England in Notre-Dame. At the same time, the

people had to fight the outbreak of terrible epidemics of plague. Louis XI who signed the peace treaty with England gave royal authority a stronger basis and encouraged national unity, creating an economic redevelopment which was to last until the 16th century with the establishment of the first French printing works in the Sorbonne, the building of the Town Hall, the rebuilding of the Louvre and the development of a whole range of artistic and cultural activities. The monarchs may have had a marked preference for the gentle banks of the Loire where they built their castles, but Paris already had its first bards. The only discordant note in this century was the bitter struggle against the Protestants with its sinister climax, the St. Bartholomew's Day Massacre on the night of 24th August 1572. Henri IV, who had decided that « Paris was worth going to Mass for », abjured his Calvinist beliefs. He had the place Royale (now the place des Vosges), the place Dauphine and the Pont-Neuf built and the town modernised (the streets were cobbled). Until then, its mediaeval appearance had hindered the movements of an already-large population (approx. 300, 000 inhabitants). Renaissance architecture blossomed in the building of private mansions in which stone replaced plaster. The Ile Saint-Louis was connected to the Ile la Cité by a number of bridges and building started on the wharves. The Marais became the setting for luxurious aristocratic residences. In the reign of Louis XIII, Paris became a veritable administrative, political and cultural centre, and in 1635 it gained the Académie Francaise. Royal squares and triumphal arches ensured that the reigns of Louis XIV and Louis XV were not forgotten and other major building ventures also saw the light of day—the Invalides, the

The Forum des Halles.

The Louvre pyramid.

Observatory. the Military Academy and the Pantheon. The revolutionaries of 1789 sought out all traces of despotism in the streets of Paris and caused devastation which spared neither monuments nor works of art. It was to continue until the days of Napoleon. In honour of the great military victories of the Empire, he had the Vendôme Column, the Arc de Triomphe, and the triumphal Carrousel Arch erected. The new personalities favoured the gardens of the Palais-Royal and the public parks with their presence, and crowded to the numerous receptions and balls. The sewers were to be continued throughout the 18th century as

part of major projects instigated by Napoleon 111 and the Prefect of the Seine, Baron Haussmann, whose town planning was to make a city of more than one and a half million inhabitants a healthier place to live. The place de l'Étoile, the opera house, the Buttes-Chaumont, and the Bois de Boulogne all sprang up at the end of the new major roads. Baltard extended the Halles (covered market). The villages on the outskirts of the city, including Montmartre, became part of a Paris that was divided into 20 wards. The fall of the Empire and the capitulation to the Prussians at Sedan led to the terrible riots of the Commune with their

series of disasters and renewed destruction (the Town Hall, the Palace, the Vendôme Column, etc.). Yet a revival was born out of the ashes. During the Third Republic, a number of buildings were erected—the Sacré-Cœur, the Grand and Petit Palais, the Trocadéro, the Eiffel Tower, etc. Not to mention the first underground railway line at the time of the great World Fairs. After the bombing raids of the two World Wars and an occupation that lasted for four years, the Liberation in 1944 set the city back on the road to a freedom which has been sought for more than two thousand years. When François Mitterand took over

The Arc de Triomphe.

the presidence of the Republic in 1981, a new architectural era began - the period of "Major Works" (redeployment of the Louvre, opening of the Orsay Art Gallery, construction of the Institute of Arab Culture and Civilisation, the Bastille Opera House and the Arche de la Défense, the redevelopment of the Villette District, the transfer and modernisation of the Ministry of the Economy and Finance). "Giving birth to the future means blending dreams and knowledge, selecting imagination, training and adaptation to a future for which, although we cannot predict it, we can pave the way" (F. Mitterand).

8

THE ARC DE TRIOMPHE

The arch stands on the very top of the Chaillot Hill. Based on the arches of Antiquity, 63 ft. high and 146 ft. wide, it is bigger than the ones in Imperial Rome. It reigns supreme on a square which, lying as it does at the junction of several roads, was known as the Étoile de Chaillot (Star of Chaillot) as far back as 1730. The Arc was designed by **Chalgrin** in 1806, on the orders of Napoleon who wanted to pay homage to the Great Army. Goust took over the work, which came to a halt with the downfall of the Empire — it was not to be completed until **1836**. The inauguration was held on 26th July of that year, in the presence of Louis who was celebrating the anniversary of his recovery of the throne. Once the monarchy had been restored, it was decided to dedicate the monument to the memory of those who had fallen for the Republic in 1792 — among whom were both royalists and Imperial soldiers. The 128 names of battles and 660 names of generals carved on the façades were then divided equally between the armies of the two régimes.

Since then, the Arc de Triomphe has never ceased to pay homage to patriots. In 1840, the emperor's ashes were placed there during a grandiose ceremony. Many great men were given the final honours here — in 1877, Gambetta in 1882, Victor Hugo in 1886, Lazare Carnot in 1889, Mac-Mahon in 1893, Foch in 1929, Joffre in 1931, Leclerc in 1947 and de Lattre de Tassigny in 1952. Napoleon III passed triumphantly beneath the arch when he took power on 2nd December 1852. The victorious army paraded through it on 14th July 1919, 26th August 1944 and 18th June 1945. On 1th November 1920, the **Tomb of an Unknown Soldier** who fell during the Battle of Verdun was transferred there and honoured as a symbol of all the soldiers killed during the First World War. And three years later, a **flame** perpetuating their memory was lit in a bronze bowl. It is rekindled every evening at 6.30 and is never allowed to go out.

On the side overlooking the Champs-Élysées, the arch is decorated with haut-reliefs. On the right is « The Departure of the Volunteers » (or « The Marseillaise ») by Rude; on the left « Triumph, » carved by Cortot in 1810. The other side has two

The Grand Arch (overleaf).
The "Marseillaise" on the Arc de Triomphe.

sculptures by Etex — « Resist-ance » (1814) and « Peace » (1815). The shields along the frieze on the attic bear the names of military victories from the days of the Republic and the Empire.

The **place Charles-de -Gaulle - Étoile**, designed out by Hittorff and Haussmann and measuring 780 ft. in diameter is surrounded by Second Empire residences. Radiating from it are twelve superb avenues, most of them laid out in the 19th-century. The one hundred stone milestones around the arch are a reminder of Napoleon's One Hundred Days in power when he returned from the island of Elba.

ARCHE DE LA DEFENSE
(La Défense R.E.R. station)

In 1982, an international com-petition was launched to find a design for a monument to be pla-ced in Tête-Défense. It was to express the architecture of today but include amenities that would be of general interest. Standing at the prow of the vast 395-acre business district known as La Défense, the "Manhattan of Fran-ce", the **monumental arch** made of Carrare marble was completed in time for the festivities marking the bicentenary of the French Revolution. It was designed by a Danish architect named Otto von Spreckelsen who, in 1986 just one year before he died, passed the work on to his lifelong asso-ciate Paul Andreu. Of all the major projects of this last decade, this was the only one to have met with universal approval. The Arch completes the layout of the Défense District, and is its most prestigious building.

This open "cube" 364 ft. high is supported by 12 piles reaching

down to a depth of 97 ft. The interior of the monument is 293 ft. high, and 227 ft. wide and deep.

Below ground level, there are a large number of constructions at this point (motorway, suburban rail link, railway etc.). Because of this, the great arch had to be tur-ned slightly compared to the his-torical axis, which is somewhat reminiscent of the offsetting of the square courtyard in the Lou-vre. But the slightly "staggered" setting seems to give the monu-ment a more "humane" appearan-ce and, more importantly, allows its full volume to be seen from the centre of Paris .

The gables are covered in grey-veined white marble while the external walls are made of

The Grand Arch.

The Défense District.

grey marble and glass. The honeycombed inner walls and the inside of the roof are covered in aluminium.

The Grand Arch is not an empty shell (there is 936,120 sq. ft. of office space in the 35 storeys of the two vertical walls). It includes not only offices but also the Ministry of Works, Housing and Transport.

The **roof-terrace**, which has an area of almost 2 1/2 acres, is given over to the Ark of Fraternity (or the International Foundation for Human Rights and Development) whose president is Claude Cheysson. The meeting rooms and conference halls are lit from four open-air patios, each with an area of 4,304 sq. ft.

Panoramic lifts take visitors up and down.

The base and sub-base house vast halls used for exhibitions and other events.

"The **Clouds**", explains Paul Andrieu, "have practical functions first and foremost - they provide shelter and a windbreak (...). They are vital for the Cube because they create a link between the monument, the surrounding buildings of the CNIT and the hills. Moreover, they give an identity to the esplanade in front of the Arch".

Originally designed to be made of glass, they were finally built of teflon canvas stretched over a network of cables.

"In fact, they act like trees in front of a building. Like trees, they bring a feeling of density into the space, they break up the view, giving it a wider perspect-

ive, creating distances, incidents, and surprises. And last but not least, the clouds bring a human scale to a space that has none other".

The monument, which was an architectural and technical challenge, had a duty to become part of other, more aesthetic challenges. **Works of art** are being created at the present time, viz. :

- Jean Dewasne's fresco (measuring 292 ft. by 227 ft.) which is to cover the south wall of the Arch;

- a huge pavement representing the circle of the zodiac, in the patios on the roofs (by J.P. Raynaud);

- a wire and metal composition in the Japanese style to be set up near the Grande Arche by Aïko Miyawaki.

THE BASTILLE
(Bastille metro station)

Built in the 14th-century, this was originally a mere **fortress** defending access to the Saint-Antoine Gate and affording protection for the royal residence of Saint-Paul's. It became a **state prison** in the reign of Louis XII in the 16th-century. However, when on the 14th July 1789, the rioters attacked it in order to provide themselves with weaponry, it was almost empty. Governor Launay and his Swiss guards had only seven prisoners in their charge. Gone were the days of the victims of the royal arbitrator and the sealed letters of imprisonment that incarcerated a Voltaire, a Marmontel or some other great nobleman tracked down because of his political ideas. Not that this mattered — the downfall of the Bastille was seen as a symbol. Its demolition was ordered and carried out by 700 labourers who worked for a little over two months. With the stones from the prison, people made a few miniatures of the « execrable fortress » which were then sent to the provinces in order to exorcise its very memory. The remainder were used in new buildings (including the Concorde Bridge).

In its place, Napoleon had the idea of a fountain in the shape of an elephant but the project was soon abandoned and all that remains is the base which, since 1840, has born a **bronze column** topped by a statue of the **Spirit of Liberty**. It was in commemoration of another month of July, the 1830 Revolution, that Louis-Philippe had the monument erected; on it are inscribed in gilded letters the names of the Parisians killed during the riots and buried in underground tombs.

The Place de la Bastille.

The Pompidou Centre.

BEAUBOURG
(Georges-Pompidou Centre)
(Rambuteau metro station)

It was Georges Pompidou who, in 1969, had the idea of making the old Beaubourg plateau (then undergoing complete renovation) a major centre of culture and the arts, a sort of « Luna Park of contemporary culture, » as it was described, « a way of linking knowledge of the arts to democracy », as Jacques Chirac put it.

The project submitted by Renzo Piano and Richard Rogers of Ove Arup and Partners was chosen over its 680 rivals. They had designed a gigantic building which aroused passionate criticism. Built entirely of steel and glass, it is 180 yds. long, 65 yds. wide,

and 130 ft. high. The beams have a 162 ft. span despite their height of only 10 ft. and each of them weighs 70 metric tonnes. The square, which is strictly reserved for pedestrians, covers an area of over 103,000 sq.m.

Since 31st January 1977, the date of its inauguration, the **National Centre for Contemporary Art** (C.N.A.C.) has annually opened its doors to thousands of visitors (more than the Eiffel Tower) who crowd onto the escalators serving the five floors. The centre comprises the Museum of Modern Art, the Centre of Industrial Creativity, the Public News Library, the Institute for acoustic-musical Research and Coordination (I.R.C.A.M.) and the film library.

BIBLIOTHÈQUE NATIONALE
The National Library
(Richelieu-Drouot metro station)

The royal library, the first-ever public library, was set up by **Mazarin** who, having purchased the Tubeuf Mansion, had François Mansart build the two galleries —the « Mansart » and the « Mazarine ». They housed the Cardinal's private library and objets d'art (which were transferred to the Mazarine Library in the Palais de l'Institut on his death). The oldest section contains **manuscripts written by the Kings of France**, in particular Charles V. With the development of the printing press and the introduction of the registration of copyright in the reign of François I, the collections were regularly increased.

The library became national and, during the Revolution, acquired works confiscated elsewhere. Today, the departments of **Printed Matter, Manuscripts,** and **Engravings** (the largest and oldest collection of its kind anywhere in the world), **Maps and plans, Music, and Medals and Antiques**, comprise a total of 10 million books, 400,000 periodicals, and 12 million engravings and photographs, in an area of 16,500 sq.m. The modern iron and glass architecture in the Reading Room was the work of Labrouste in the 19th-century. The glass roofs let in a maximum of light. The Mansart Gallery was restored in 1938, the Mazarine in 1977. They house exhibitions that are open to the public. The Courtyard was laid out in the 18th-century by the architect Robert de Cotte.

The Arc de Triomphe seen from the Champs-Elysées (overleaf).

The Pompidou Centre.

THE CHAMPS-ELYSEES
(Champs-Elysées Clémenceau metro station)

These days it is difficult to imagine that, in the 17th century, the "most famous avenue anywhere in the world" was nothing more than marshland and scrub. In 1760, Colbert asked Le Nôtre to create an "esplanade" beyond the Tuileries with elms in the hedgerows as far as what we now know as the Rond-Point. The avenue became known as the Champs-Elysées in 1709, was extended to the future Place de l'Etoile in 1724, and reached the present Porte Maillot in 1774. At that time, however, it was little more than a piece of rough country into which few dared to venture. In the early 19th century, balls, circuses, and puppet theatres attracted the first wave of strollers. It was, though, not until the Second Empire that the avenue really came alive - it became the meeting-place for the rich who rode in their tilburies, frequented the café-concerts (e.g. the Alcazar) and the restaurants, danced the mazurka in the Mabille Dance Hall in « Widow's Avenue » (now the avenue Montaigne), applauded shows in the Colisée, and flocked to the Winter Gardens or the Flower Castle to see or be seen. Trade developped, town planning progressed (the six lonely houses of 1800 were a thing of the past), and the avenue acquired the appearance it was to keep for all time. The **Rond-Point** laid out by Le Nôtre, flanked by flowers and fountains, divides the avenue into two sections. The **south end** stretches down to the Place de la Concorde in a series of paths and **gardens** from whose midst rise

The Champs-Elysées seen from the Arc de Triomphe.

the Petit and Grand Palais, the Second Empire mansions housing the « Figaro » newspaper and « Jours de France » magazine, several famous theatres (Espace Cardin, Marigny), and a number of great restaurants. On the **north** side, the 230 ft. wide avenue runs up to the Arc de Triomphe. Here the aristocratic mansions give way to luxury shops, shopping precincts (Élysées Rond-Point, Claridge), exclusive cinemas, airlines, banks, and a plethora of cafés and drugstores, where there are crowds of people all year long. Of the magnificence of last century, only the sumptuous Païva Residence remains. Païva was a Polish courtesan who held at homes at No. 25 for V.I.P.'s from the smart set of the day.

The avenue des Champs-Élysées is still a symbol for the nation as a whole. Parisians gathered there to celebrate the Liberation of their city and every 14th July the major branches of the armed forces parade down it with great solemnity.

THE COMÉDIE-FRANÇAISE
(Palais-Royal metro station)

In 1680, Louis XIV sent a sealed letter ordering the merger of the theatrical company left by

A portrait of Molière.

Molière when he died seven years earlier and the one that used the Burgundy Residence. This was the birth of the Comédie-Française but it was also the beginning of numerous peregrinations for the company. It first took up residence near the rue Guénégaud before moving to what we now know as the rue de l'Ancienne Comédie, then to the Tuileries Palace and later to the Théâtre Français (now the Odéon). Political events, which often provided inspiration for the theatre of the day and which on the other hand could make or break the company's very existence, brought about its division in 1793, the Royalists remaining in the Théâtre-Français while the Republicans moved to the Palais-Royal auditorium. It was then called the « Théâtre de la République » and was used as an « Old Time Music Hall ».

Molière and Ionesco

Very quickly the Comédie-Française, which had already ensured the success of Classical tragedies or comedies from authors named Racine, Corneille and Molière, decided on a high-quality repertoire.

Although the delicate subtleties of playful flirting said little to 18th-century audiences, Goldoni and Beaumarchais enjoyed outright success and brought to the public's attention the talent of Talma, who was to become the « Emperor's actor ». With « Hernani », Victor Hugo was to set off a memorable battle opposing Classicists and Romantics, preparing the way for people like Musset. On a lighter note, the turn of the century saw plays by Labiche, Courteline, and Mirabeau. In the 20th century, the Comédie-Française provided the consecration of works by Montherlant, Claudel, Anouilh, Ionesco and Beckett. In all, 3,000 plays and some 800 authors are on the company's repertoire which has been open to new authors and directors over the past few years.

Full members

In 1861, a royal decree created the status of the 27 actors and actresses of the day who received an allowance based on company profits. Today the grant-aided Comédie-Française Co. consists of full members, some of whom are co-opted, who nominate those due an allowance for a period of one year. Both groups are obliged to reserve their talent exclusively for the company's activities—apart from playing in national theatres or elsewhere with the agreement of the administrator. It is this obligation which most often prompts actors to leave. The theatre's auditoriums still ring with the glory of great names like Rachel, Mlle Mars, Sarah Bernhardt and Cécile Sorel, Pierre Fresnay, Madeleine Renaud, Jean-Louis Barraud, Marie Marquet, Pierre Dux or Jacques Charon, to name but a few. All of them were very worthy successors of Molière and Armande Béjart.

A veritable business

This, then, is the Comédie-Française which today employs 372 people in maintenance, decoration, administration, security or office work. The 68 actors provide 450 performances per year, some of them twice in one day. A management committee of full members presided over by an administrator desi-

The stage in the Comédie Française.

The Conciergerie.

gnated for 3 years by the government (with responsibility for the reading committee) ensures the smooth running of the company.

Maintaining the national heritage

A **library** protects the past of an institution that is three hundred years old, and a number of precious collections which have not yet been brought together under one museum roof prove how rich its history is.

The building

The Comédie-Française building, dating from 1786-1790 and designed by **Victor Louis** who was also the architect of Bordeaux' Theatre, is six storeys high. A colonnade runs along the ground floor. A metal framework has been incorporated in the building to reduce the fire risk. It was Prosper Chabrol who restored the roof and south façade in the 19th century. The Richelieu Auditorium, which can seat 892, is decorated with a ceiling painted by

Albert Besnard in 1913. The foyer contains a row of busts. The ones of Voltaire and Molière were carved by Houdon.

THE CONCIERGERIE
(Cité metro station)

In the 14th century, Philip the Fair extended the Law Courts and had the Gothic buildings of the Conciergerie erected, placing it under the responsibility of the "concierge", or King's governor, who fulfilled both a legal and a financial role. In the 15th century, trade developed in the shops along the galleries, before being replaced by dark gaol cells that have remained in people's memories because they were used to incarcerate the thousands of prisoners condemned by the Revolutionary Tribunal - among them,

The Conciergerie.

Marie-Antoinette, the poet André Chénier, and the politicians Camille Desmoulins, Marat, Saint-Just and Lavoisier. Most of them kept their appointment with the guillotine, which worked non-stop on the place de la Concorde, de la Bastille or de la Nation between 1792 and 1794.

Overlooking the Seine are four old towers. The square **Clock Tower** has housed the first public clock in Paris since the 14th century. The present clock was carved in the 16th century by Germain Pilon but has been remade since that time. The other three towers are all round. The oldest one is the **Bonbec Tower** dating from the mid 13th century, where prisoners were often tortured. The **Silver Tower** and **Caesar's Tower** are identical.

The restoration work undertaken in the Guardroom in the 19th century was an attempt to live down the existence of the prison graves. The impressively-large Chamber of the Gentlemen-of-Arms next door was used as a dining hall in the Middle Ages. In the nearby kitchens equiped with four fireplaces, substantial meals were prepared for 2,000-3,000 guests. In the so-called "**Rue de Paris**", the executioner Sanson's domaine during the Revolution, "Monsieur de Paris" (the public executioner) used to squeeze in all the "pailleux" (or "straw yokels") i.e. prisoners who were not wealthy enough to be accommodated in an individual cell. The dispensers and victims of his rudimentary justice used to be seen in the **Prisoners' Gallery**. The dungeon in which Marie-Antoinette spent her last two months was made into an expiatory chapel in 1816. It lay next to the chapel where the Girondins were held before being taken to the scaffold in that same year, 1793, and it overlooks the **Womens' Courtyard** where poor and wealthy alike used to mingle.

THE PLACE DE LA CONCORDE
(Concorde metro station)

Louis XV bought this former piece of marshland and made it over to the aldermen of Paris who undertook to lay out a square in his honour. The design project was

The Place de la Concorde.

The Place de la Concorde.

entrusted to **Jacques-Ange Gabriel**, who created an octagon with an area of 84,000 sq. m., flanked by vast ditches. At the same time, he laid out the rue Royale, erecting on each side of the junction magnificent palaces whose colonnades are reminiscent of the one Perrault built in the Louvre. The palace on the right-hand side was used as a royal warehouse (it was from there that the Crown Jewels were stolen); it now houses the Ministry of Navy. The one on the left quickly became a private residence. It is now occupied by the Automobile Club de France and the prestigious Hôtel Crillon

(the family of that name continued to live there until 1904).

An equestrian statue of Louis XV sculpted by Bouchardon and Pigalle stood in the middle of the square named after the king until the Revolution when it was replaced by a statue of Liberty. A guillotine was also set up here, and its victims, more than 1,100 of them in all, included Louis XVI and Marie-Antoinette, Charlotte Corday, Danton, Robespierre, and Mme Roland whose famous sentence, « Liberty, how many crimes are committed in thy name », has gone down in History. The square was renamed

« Concorde » in 1795 in the days of the Directory and was given its final layout after the Restoration of the Monarchy, mainly thanks to the architect Jacques Hittorff. In 1836, the **obelisk** presented to Louis-Philippe by the Viceroy of Egypt, Mohammed Ali, replaced the previous succession of statues. Taken from the temple at Luxor, this pink syenite monument, that is over 74 ft. tall with a weight of 230 metric tonnes, recounts the feats of Ramses II in hieroglyphics. The granite pedestal is a reminder of the long and difficult journey undertaken by the engineer Lebas who was responsible for shipping the obelisk back to France. The **two fountains,** erected between 1836 and 1846, are 29 ft. tall and are reminiscent of the ones on St. Peter's Square in Rome. They are symbols of river and maritime navigation. The ditches laid out by Gabriel were filled in after some one hundred people were trampled to death during an evening celebration in 1770. There are eight statues representing France's major towns—Petitot carved the ones of Lyons and Marseilles, Callouet was asked to sculpt Nantes and Bordeaux, Cortot did Rouen and Brest, and Pradier made Lille and Strasburg (Juliette Drouet was the model for the last one).

The **horses** that Guillaume Coustou had carved for the drinking troughs at **Marly** and which had stood at the entrance to the Champs-Élysées since 1795 have recently been replaced by replicas. Threatened by pollution and vibrations from the Underground system, they are now enjoying a well-earned rest in the Louvre. Coysevox' **winged horses** decorating the entrance to the Tuileries were likewise replaced in the spring of 1985. The **Concorde Bridge** provides an unbroken view from the Madeleine Church to the Palais-Bourbon. When it was built (it was completed in 1791), the old engineer Perronet used stone from the Bastille which was then being demolished.

THE MILITARY ACADEMY
(Ecole Militaire metro station)

This is the oldest building on the Champ-de-Mars. Madame de Pompadour and the financier Pâris-Duverney wanted to provide military training for the sons of poor or meritorious officers. The idea of the academy was born, and it was built by **Gabriel** between 1751 and 1772. By the time young Bonaparte attended it in 1784, it had already been the « Cadet College » for several years. He left it as a second-lieutenant in an artillery regiment. He became a General, then Emperor, and accommodated his personal guard in the buildings as they had lost their original purpose during

The Military Academy.

The Petit Palais.

the Revolution. Transformed into barracks, the Academy has since 1878 been the War College, the National Defence Institute, and the Supply Services College.

The **central section** is built along sumptuously Classical lines (dating from the 18th century) with eight Corinthian columns below a decorated pediment and a quadrangular dome. To each side are buildings from the Second Empire. The **central courtyard** opens onto the place Fontenoy which no longer bears any resemblance to its original 18th century appearance.

Inside, the Louis XVI-style chapel is decorated with an altar designed by Gabriel. The great staircase has a wrought-iron handrail and the Marshal's Salon has its original wood-panelling.

THE GRAND PALAIS AND THE PETIT PALAIS
(Champs-Elysées Clémenceau metro station)

Built for the 1900 World Fair, the two halls are proof of an often ill-accepted renewed interest in town planning. The imposing architecture using only stone and iron is a magnificent Baroque style reminiscent of the Opera House. Quadriga stand guard at the four corners of the **Grand Palais**. Designed by Louvet, the hall has an Ionic colonnade 780 ft. long and 65 ft. high while the interior stands beneath a vast flattened dome. Its 5,000 sq. m. used to cater for a variety of exhibitions such as the Motor Show, the Ideal Homes Exhibition or the F.I.A.C. (International Modern Art Show); today, people go to see temporary art exhibitions in the National Galleries and to visit the Palace of Discovery. The **Petit Palais**, which is the Municipal Art Gallery,

The Grand Palais.

was the work of Charles Girault. It houses a permanent collection of rare objects dating from the Middle Ages up to the 19th century, as well as prints and pottery.

The entrance to the Invalides stands on the other side of the **Alexander III Bridge**. Completed in 1900, it bears all the hallmarks of the audacity and abundance of the Gay Nineties. It was inaugurated by Nicolas II, the son of Tsar Alexander III, and set the seal on the Franco-Russian alliance. Its metal arch with its 348 ft. span weighs approximately 5,300 metric tonnes. It is decorated with allegorical figures and flourishes that are well in keeping with the artistic taste of the day.

THE CLUNY MANSION
(Saint-Michel or Odéon metro station)

Three stages in its history led to the development of its three spheres of interest. Recent archaeological digs whose most important discoveries were consoles in the shapes of the prows of ships proved that c. 215 A.D. public baths stood on this spot; they were for the use of the rich boatmen of the Parisian corporations and were demolished some sixty years later by the Barbarians. Only the « frigidarium » (literally « a cool place ») stands out above the ruins. It measures 65 ft. by 36 ft.and is 46 ft. high. Its walls are almost 7 ft. thick. The **Seine Boatmen's Pillar**, uncovered in 1711 beneath the chancel in Notre-Dame, is the oldest piece of sculpture in Paris. It was probably part of the temple that originally stood on the site of the cathedral and which the ferrymen had dedicated to Jupiter in the early years of the Christian era. It is one of the major exhibits in the **Archaeological Museum** housing the discoveries made during these archaeological digs. It also contains the 21 heads of Biblical kings carved in the 13th century and severely damaged during the Revolution.

In 1334, Pierre de Châlus, Abbot of Cluny, acquired the site and the ruins on which he built a mansion to accommodate the abbots from the college opposite the Sorbonne erected by the monks of Cluny. It was rebuilt in

The "Lady with the Unicorn" tapestry in the Cluny Museum.

The Cluny Residence.

1485 by Jacques of Amboise. Although it underwent restoration during last-century, its crenelated walls, turrets, skylights, mullioned windows and splendid balustrade still make it a fine example of civil Flamboyant architecture in the Middle Ages. In 1515, the mansion provided shelter for the « White Queen » (white being the colour of royal mourning), Mary of England, Louis XII 's widow, while in the 17th century it accommodated papal nuncios and Mazarin. It was sold off as State property during the Revolution. In 1833, **collector** called Alexandre du Sommerard used it to house his fabulous collections of mediaeval objets d'art which the State purchased on his death in 1844 in order to found a museum.

The museum provides vital information about life and art in the pre-Renaissance period. Visitors can admire the votive-crowns of Visigoth kings (7th century), the magnificent golden altar from Basle cathedral, the Deploration of the Cross reredos (a 15th-century masterpiece), illuminated manu scripts, enamel-work, pieces of gold and silver, and more importantly tapestries including the famous « **Lady with the Unicorn** » dating from the 15th century. It is not known who made the six tapestries representing the Five Senses and a sixth canvas said to illustrate the renunciation of the world. The lion and unicorn emblem stand out on a red background of flowers on which there is a blue island.

The central pilaster in the chapel (formerly the Abbots' private chapel) bears a Flamboyant Gothic vault. Statues of the Amboise family stand in niches above consoles. The tapestry in the chapel comes from Auxerre Cathedral and illustrates the Legend of St. Stephen.

THE MINT
Hôtel des Monnaies
(Pont-Neuf metro station)

Jacques-Denis Antoine built the Mint between 1771 and 1777 on the site of the Conti Mansion. It lay parallel to the Seine rather than perpendicular to it as tradition demanded.

The 390-foot facade has a fore-part in the centre comprising five arches and an attic. The six allegorical statues represent Abundance, Peace, Trade, Strength, Justice and Prudence. The huge door bears the mark of Louis XIV and is decorated with a bronze tympanum. The central section in the rue Guénégaud has statues of the four elements — Earth, Water, Air and Fire.

The Mint.

Since 1973, no coins and medals have been minted in the workshops here; they are minted in Pessac in Gironde (S.W. France). A **permanent exhibition** contains collections of items and coins, some of which date from the time of the Ancient Gauls.

CITY HALL
(Hôtel-de-Ville metro station)

The history of France is closely linked to that of its capital city and the disagreements opposing central government and the municipality of Paris have often had nationwide repercussions.

The **town council** dates back to the 13th-century. The « Hanseatic League », an Association of Watermen, was then a flourishing corporation with a monopoly on river traffic along the Seine. In 1260, St. Louis gave its deans and jurors responsability for running the town. The Dean of Guilds assisted by elected aldermen (magistrates) and designated councillors gave the town the motto of the blue and red ship which appeared on their own coat-of-arms, « Fluctuat nec mergitur » (« It floats but does not sink »). At that time, the town council met on the place du Châtelet. In 1357 the Dean of Guilds, Etienne Marcel, had its meeting-place transferred to the **place de Grève** and he fomented a revolt, the first against royal authority. However, it took more than that to worry the square on which public executions were carried out — hangings or beheadings for common law crimes, drawing and quartering for crimes of lèse-majesté. The Count of Montgomery, Henri II's unintentional murderer, and Ravaillac who assassinated Henri IV both died in this way. In the Middle Ages, the square was a meeting-

place for the jobless (hence the expression « faire grève » meaning « to go on strike ») as well as the setting for festivities.

In 1533, on the site of the **House of Pillars** which had collapsed, François I laid the foundation stone of a new building begun by Dominique de Cortone but not completed until the 17th-century. In 1789, the revolutionaries took this strategic place by storm and elected a mayor — Jean-Sylvain Bailly. Louis XVI was obliged to wear a cockade in the colours of the town (red and blue) to which La Fayette had recently added the royal white. Robespierre found asylum and tried to commit suicide there when he fell into disgrace. Bonaparte had the building redecorated and the **Throne Room** restored. He organised a new administrative structure for the capital, thenceforth subdivided into 12 wards on which the Prefect of the Seine and the Chief of Police kept a watchful eye. In 1832, « believing that the place de Grève could no longer be used for executions since generous citizens gloriously spilt their blood there for the sake of the nation », the Prefect of the Seine decided not to abolish the executions as requested by the 4,000 signitaries of a petition, but to transfer them to Saint-Jacques. During the troubles of 1848, Lamartine who was then a member of the provisional government, supported the three-coloured flag « which has never been further than the Champ de Mars ». By the 1867 World Fair, extension work on the building was almost complete, at least inside. Balls and banquets could then cater for a cosmopolitan collection of V.I.P.'s amidst sumptuous surroundings (some of which were the work of Delacroix and Ingres). Fire, though, destroyed the Town Hall during the Paris Commune in

City Hall.

1871. The country became a Republic once and for all, yet it took a century (1977) for Paris to gain another mayor. In 1945, the Town of Paris received the Cross

The banks of the Seine and the Ile Saint-Louis (overleaf).

of the Companion of the Liberation from the hands of General de Gaulle.

The present **Neo-Renaissance** City Hall was built in the years 1874-1882 to designs by the architects Ballu and Deperthes based on plans drawn in the 16th-century by Cortone. There are 136 statues representing famous people, including Etienne Marcel, around the outside of the building. The interior is a fine example of Third Republic art.

ILE SAINT-LOUIS
(Pont-Marie metro station)

At the beginning of the 17thcentury, Louis XIII took up one of Henri IV 's projects and decided to end the isolation of the two islands, Ile Notre-Dame and Ile aux Vaches (literally « Cows' Island », the place where the animals were put out to graze and where tournaments and duels were held in the Middle Ages), by connecting them to terra firma by two bridges. The work, lasting from 1627 to 1660, created a new urban district criss-crossed by streets on which Le Vau built some very fine mansions for high-ranking statesmen, intendants, financiers and magistrates.

A few of the 17th and 18th-century residences are still standing, including the **Lauzun Mansion**. Built for an army contractor, it had several prestigious occupants in addition to the Duc de Lauzun, Louis XIV's courtier, including the poets Théophile Gautier and Charles Baudelaire. It now belongs to Paris Town Council. The interior decoration is quite remarkable.

In the 17th-century, the Lambert Mansion belonged to a president of the Parliament, Lambert de Thorigny. Built like the previous mansion by Le Vau, it was decorated by Le Sueur and Le Brun. It once accommodated Rousseau and Voltaire.

St. Louis' Church was begun by Le Vau in 1664 but was not completed until 1726. It is noteworthy mainly for its mediaeval and Renaissance objets d'art, sculptures, ceramics and pieces of enamelwork which it either saved during the Revolution or collected in the l9th century.

THE INSTITUTE OF FRANCE
(Pont-Neuf or Saint-Germain-des-Prés metro station)

On his death, Mazarin left a very large sum of money for the setting up of a college to cater for some sixty pupils from the newly-acquired provinces of Artois, Piedmont, Alsace and Roussillon — hence its original name, the **Four-Nations College**. The building work (1663-1693) was entrusted to Louis Le Vau who was also working on the Louvre. He demolished the ramparts dating from the reign of Philip Augustus and the famous Nesle Tower (which had inspired many

The Institut de France.

a legend) and erected this concave façade flanked by two wings about a chapel topped by the celebrated dome (the cardinal's arms are carved on it).

Mazarin's sumptuous **tomb** of white and black marble, one of Coysevox' masterpieces dating from 1689, was placed in the vestibule of the chapel. The allegorical figures, also made of bronze, are shown with their mouths tight shut as a reminder, it is said, of the silence imposed by the cardinal on Prudence, Abundance, and Loyalty, the qualities they represent. To the left of the dome is a door leading into the courtyard. The West portico opens onto the **Mazarin Library**, some of the rich collection being Mazarin's own. He left the books at the same time as the « shelves, tables, cupboards, benches and seats ». The second courtyard, originally the kitchen yard, still contains an **old well** decorated with wrought-iron work.

The Four-Nations College became a detention centre in 1793 and thereafter suffered a variety of ups-and-downs until Napoleon installed the Institute of France in it. Since 1795, it had comprised the Académie française, founded by Richelieu in 1635, the Academy of Inscriptions and Belles Lettres, the Academy of Moral and Political Sciences, the Fine Arts Academy, and the Academy of Science. The chapel was then chosen as the setting for the installation cere-monies for newly-elected members of the Académie française. For every election, which is subject to the approval of the Head of State, the Forty members, who recently voted for a woman, dress in the green ceremonial costume with the cocked hat, cape and sword. And every week the « Immortals » as they

The Institut du Monde Arabe.

are known (the Académie's motto is « To immortality ») collaborate on a new edition of the « Dictionary of the French Language. » Most of them are writers but there are a few historians, members of the clergy, army officers and even film producers.

INSTITUT DU MONDE ARABE
(Institute of Arab Civilisation and Culture)
(Cardinal-Lemoine metro station)

Although first planned in 1974, the Institute was not finally

37

The courtyard in the Invalides (above).

The Invalides (opposite).

And the south wall is designed to resemble the traditional "moucharaby" (a balcony in front of a window closed off by latticework). Thousands of photoelectric cells filter the light streaming through the windows.

The **interior** houses a museum on five floors (the oldest items on display come from the Louvre but there is also a Modern Art section), a library with 40,000 books and 800 periodicals in Arabic, English and French, a documentation centre, a Current Events Room (containing the most up-to-date books), and a Sound and Picture Section. The auditorium in the basement can seat 360. On the top floor is a restaurant with a panoramic view over Paris.

The IMA houses numerous temporary exhibitions, many of them lavish, and all of them well worth seeing.

THE INVALIDES
(Invalides metro station)

On the huge **esplanade** (540 yds. by 270 yds.) designed by Robert de Cotte and laid out between 1704 and 1720 stand the gigantic and austere buildings that form the Invalides. The **residence** was built in 1671 by Libéral Bruant on Louis XIV's orders and was to be used to accommodate soldiers who had been wounded in the service of their sovereign. Nowadays, **museums** (the Army Museum, the Plans and Relief Maps Museum, and the Order of the Liberation Museum) perpetuate the military vocation of this temple of heroism in which may a soldier has been buried. The demolition of additional buildings and the restoration work carried out under Malraux' leadership have

founded until 1980. The cosignatories of the project are France and some twenty Arab countries and each is contributing an equal sum to this attempt to bridge the gap between Western and Arab-Moslem cultures.

Built between the R.Seine and the Science Faculty in Jussieu, the nine-storey building (covering 289,444 sq.ft.) was the winner of an architectural competition judged in 1981. The designers were Jean Nouvel, Pierre Soria, Gilbert Lezènes and the team of Architecture Studio. The building, "a combination of glass, metal and light", was completed in 1987.

The transparent west wall shows the shelving inside, hence the Centre's nickname, the "Book Tower". The north wall reflects the 19th-century buildings on the Ile Saint-Louis across the Seine.

The church in the Invalides stands at the end of the Alexandre III Bridge (above).

The cannon in the Invalides (below).

given the monument back all its original majesty.

In the **gardens** in front of it are bronze cannon dating from the 17th and 18th Centuries—the pieces of this « **triumphal battery** » emphasise the great days of France's military history.

In 1735, Coustou carved an equestrian statue of Louis XIV (it was restored after the Revolution) and two statues of Mars and Minerva although it is replicas which now stand at the foot of the 250 yds. long façade. A superb archway leads into the **central courtyard** (or Royal Courtyard) measuring 332 ft. by 205 ft. surrounded by four wings. The South Wing houses an 18th-century clock by Lepaute and a statue of

Napoleon dressed as the Little Corporal by Seurre (for many years it stood at the top of the Vendôme Column). The two tiers of arcaded **galleries** contain a collection of old cannon. A taxi serves as a reminder of the famous victory on the Marne in 1914.

It was Hardouin-Mansart who completed **St. Louis' Church** in 1677 in accordance with Bruant's plans. It was reserved for the soldiers but shared its altar with a chapel royal (now the Dome Church). The two chapels have been separated since 1873 by a large window. The organ designed by Mansart in the 17th century has 4,800 pipes. From the balustrade hang flags and trophies captured from the enemy. Several military dignitaries are buried in the crypt (Oudinot, Grouchy, Marceau, Kléber, Bugeaud, Mac-Mahon, Leclerc, and Juin), as are the governors of the establishment (and the daughter of one of them, Miss de Sombreuil, who saved her father from the guillotine during the Revolution), and the writer of the « Marseillaise, » Rouget de Lisle. Finally, the church has preserved the cart used for the transfer of Napoleon's ashes

The great organ in the Church of Saint-Louis-des-Invalides.

Napoleon's tomb in the Invalides.

in 1840 and the stone flags from his tomb on St. Helena.

The **Dome Church**, a later building, was mainly the work of Hardouin-Mansart. Robert de Cotte completed it in 1735. Built in a very simple Baroque style, it is a masterpiece of Classicism as seen in the Age of Enlightenment. Its layout is Jesuit. Its height, 348 feet, contains a flight of 15 steps and a facade with Doric and Corinthian columns decorated with statues of St. Louis by Coustou and Charlemagne by Coysevox (who also carved the pediment). The dome ends in an elegant lantern-tower topped by a steeple. It is decorated with garlands of flowers, trophies and other floral motifs. Since 1715, the lead sides of the roof have been regilded on several occasions. Thanks to the funds made available by the Secretary of State for Major Projects, the dome was given back its full coating of gold leaf for the festivities held on 14th July 1989.

The **interior** in the shape of a Greek cross was decorated by the greatest painters of Louis XIV's day (who also helped to decorate Versailles) e.g. Coypel who painted the vault, Visconti who decorated the high altar with its baldaquin reminiscent of the one in St. Peter's in Rome, and Etex who worked on Vauban's memorial. The paintings by Charles de La Fosse pay homage to St. Louis, the twelve Apostles and the four Evangelists.

In a wide circular **crypt**, two bronze statues keep watch over a sarcophagus made of red Karelian porphyry standing on a green Vosges granite base. This is **Napoleon's tomb**, brought back to France in the reign of Louis-Philippe and kept in St. Jerome's Chapel until Visconti had completed work on the crypt (in 1861). Six coffins of different material (tin, lead, mahogany, ebony, and oak) protect the emperor's mortal remains to whom Pradier paid further homage by carving the twelve figures symbolising Napoleon's victories. The silver urns contain his heart and entrails. Since 1969, the body of the Duc de Reichstadt, King of Rome, son of the Emperor and Marie-Louise, who died in 1832 (at the age of 21), has been laid to rest beneath a slab nearby. Several of the crypts round about contain the tombs of Bonaparte's brothers (Jérôme, King of Westphalia, and Joseph, King of Spain) as well as those of Foch, Maréchal Lyautey who pacified Morocco and was Minister of War in 1916, Turenne and Vauban, both of them Marshals under Louis XIV.

THE LOUVRE
(Palais-Royal metro station)

Seven centuries of work

Since it was first built in 1200 right up until its finest hours in the days of the Second Empire, shortly before it was demolished in fact, not with standing the period of the French Revolution, the Louvre seems to have been an indication of the history of an authority, often monarchical in nature, which attempted to ensure in turn its safety, its glory, or finally its mere existence.

Successive kings and architects (Philip Augustus, Louis IX, Charles V, François I and Pierre Lescot, Henri II and Jean Goujon, Catherine de Medici, Philibert Delorme and Jean Bullant, Henri IV, Métezeau and Androuet Du

Cerceau, Marie de Medici, Louis XIII and Jacques Lemercier, Anne of Austria, Louis XIV and Le Vau, Colbert, Bernini, Claude Perrault and Le Brun, Louis XVI, Napoleon Bonaparte, Percier and Fontaine, Napoleon III, Haussmann, Visconti and Lefuel and, nearer our own time, Malraux and Braque) have all built, demolished, restored or altered this palace, creating over seven centuries the « Great Plan for the Louvre ».

Honoured or ransacked

In the 13th century, in the absence of the King who had joined the Crusades, the Louvre was a fortress protecting the access roads to the capital. It became more « civilised » in the 14th century when Charles V the Wise built his famous library, giving

"The coronation of Napoleon" by David.

the palace its oldest artistic and cultural vocation. It was, however, abandoned for several decades by sovereigns who preferred the Saint-Paul residence or Tournelles Castle. The arrival of François I marked the passage from Gothic to Renaissance architecture which was then flourishing in Italy where the King had been at war. In 1563 Catherine de Medici, who had ordered the demolition of Tournelles where Henri II had been killed, decided on the building of a second palace, the Tuileries, which was connected to the Louvre by two galleries.

The palace and Square Courtyard were both enlarged in the 17th century. This was then the royal residence. Louis XIV organised brilliant festivities there and received his courtiers in accordance with a tradition that has remained famous. From 1678 onwards, when the royal family moved to Versailles, the Louvre fell into a « shameful state » as Voltaire described it. Although it housed several Academies and the State Opera, it was also the haunt of all sorts of undesirable elements and businesses that were far from commendable. In 1789, Louis XVI was brought back to the Tuileries by force and on his death the Revolutionaries took it over. Napoleon and Josephine settled there in 1800 and had the **place du Carrousel** laid out. The restoration work was finally finished towards the middle of the century. Fire raged through much of the Tuileries Palace during the Paris Commune. It was then decided to demolish it. The Third Republic had the two 17th-century **Marsan and Flora Wings** rebuilt.

The Louvre.

45

Artistic tradition

Charles V had given a boost to tradition with his library. François I collected the **first paintings** by masters such as Titian, Raphael and Leonardo da Vinci. Henri IV had the idea of paying artists to work in the Louvre. In the reign of Louis XIII, there were already 200 canvases ; there were 2,500 in Louis XIV's day and he ordered regular exhibitions of the paintings and sculptures. The great revolutionary ideals suggested the idea of a museum, which was finally opened to the public in 1793. With the Republic's victories in Belgium and Italy, then Napoleon's conquests, the Louvre acquired even more wealth. The resident artists were obliged to leave the palace for the Sorbonne. They were replaced by — caryatids.

When military defeat arrived, the Louvre was more or less dispossessed of its wealth. Under Louis XVIII and Charles X, however, it acquired Egyptian antiquities, soon to be joined by Greek, Assyrian and Roman collections. Purchases and gifts spiralled and diversified until the museum became one of the richest anywhere in the world with some **400,000 items** listed in its catalogue (although they are not all on show).

"The largest museum in the world"

This was the ambition for the Louvre stated by François Mitterand in 1981. On 24th September of that year, the President of the Republic announced that the Ministry of Finance would be moving to Bercy, thereby vacating the Richelieu Wing. In March 1983, an American architect of Chinese origin, Ieoh Ming Pei, was given the job of creating the modern art gallery. His preoccupation was essentially of an architectural nature - he erected a glass pyramid that was both highly sophisticated and very stark. Pei, though, had borne town planning in mind. "The Louvre had to be brought to life, for if the Louvre is dormant, it means that Paris is taking a nap". The gallery, then, had to bring together the left and right banks of the Seine.

In March 1989, the pyramid was opened to the public and the

A view from the Louvre pyramid.

The Louvre.

first stage of the work was complete. The major E.P.G.L. project, however (the Extended Louvre), will not be finished until c. 1993 the date of the museum's bicentenary) or 1995 with the opening of the Richelieu Wing, the creation of underground car parks, shopping precincts and the landscaping of the Tuileries Gardens. By redeploying its collections over 538,000 sq. ft. of exhibition space, the Louvre will indeed be the largest museum in the world.

The pyramids

With a height of 68 ft. and a weight of 200 metric tonnes, the great pyramid consists of 70 triangles and 623 (identical) diamond shapes made of "colourless" glass 20 mm thick processed by the Saint-Gobain works. It is supported by an aluminium and stainless steel structure. The building as a whole is the result of three years of construction work, and seven months of computer-assisted design by the architect, Pei, and by firms of specialists, not to mention the assistance of mountaineers who cleaned the glass! Its designer says that "It is impressive for its lack of definite style".

For some of the areas, Ieoh Ming Pei engaged the services of two famous architect-designers i.e. Richard Peduzzi (history rooms) and J-M. Willmotte (bookshop, copper engraving shop, restaurants and temporary exhibition hall).

The glass in the pyramid changes into a mirror as it reflects the water in the seven dark blue granite ponds round about, and the pavilions of the Napoleon courtyard designed by Lefuel during the reign of Napoleon III. The three small pyramids erected near the Sully, Richelieu and Denon Wings indicate the three entrances to the routes followed by visitors, as well as providing a source of light for the rooms and halls underground.

A masterpiece of Gothic architecture—the colonnade

Built in the 17th-century under the direction of Claude Perrault, the brother of the fairytale

The Arc de Triomphe du Carrousel.

The Square Courtyard in the Louvre (opposite).

*The Louvre seen from the Square du
Vert-Galant (overleaf).*

writer, it is 570 ft. long and it stands on an iron framework (a process which was to become commonplace two centuries later). The two « L » 's facing each other represent Louis XIV's cipher. The original bust of Napoleon opposite the statue of Louis XIV on the pediment designed by Lemot (1808) was replaced during the Restoration of the monarchy by one of Minerva. A winged Victory carved by Cartelier in 1807 stands above the

entrance. The ditches dug in 1965, based on plans that were unusable in the 17th-century, finally gave the building a perfect, Classical coherence. A monumental portico runs along the façade, ensuring continuity with the Square Courtyard.

The prestigious square courtyard

This is the oldest section of the Louvre, the site of the first fortress castle built in the early

13th century. Each of the wings, approximately 390 ft. long, is remarkable for its regularity and grandeur. On the west side, the wing designed by Pierre Lescot is a very fine example of Renaissance architecture. Jean Goujon and his colleagues carved beautiful allegorical motifs on it. The **Clock Pavilion** in the centre was the work of Lemercier in 1624. Above the clock, which was mounted during the Restoration of the monarchy, are caryatids

49

carved by Guérin, Poissant and Buyster. A dome tops the building as a whole.

The other three sections are Classical in style. Le Vau built the first two floors in the 17th-century, while Percier and Fontaine added a third storey in the days of the First Empire with a view to raising the wings to the same height as the colonnade. Guillaume Coustou carved the east tympanum in 1758, Claude Ramey the one on the north side in 1811, and J.-P. Sueur the one on the south side in that same period. The monograms carved on the façades are those of the monarchs who left their mark on the building project. The paving stones indicate the layout of the original Louvre Palace with its keep almost 100 ft. high and the ten towers along its walls. Passing the **Apollo Gallery** and the **Waterside Gallery** along the quays, you will come to the Flora and Marsan wings flanking the Carrousel gardens on the site of the old Tuileries Palace.

Archaeological digs carried out recently when the museum was undergoing modification uncovered the remains of the mediaeval Louvre (keep and moat of Philip Augustus' fortress and the subterranean constructions of the north and east wings of Charles V's castle which replaced it). Arachaeological crypts were created and are soon to be opened to the public. At the same time, the buildings in the courtyard were restored and concrete paving was laid down.

The Carrousel

In 1662, Louis XIV took part in one of the equestrian parades that were so popular in the 17th century, in the courtyard of the Tuileries Palace which was then given the name « Carrousel ». In 1806, Napoleon celebrated his victories in Europe. He asked Denon to build the archway designed by Percier and Fontaine similar to the one in honour of Septimus Severius in Rome. This is how this triumphal arch came into being. It is 46 ft. high and 65 ft. wide, smaller than the one on the Étoile but certainly more successful. The Château-Vieux in Meudon supplied the eight red and white marble columns that bear the statues of soldiers in the uniform of the Imperial Army. The carved bas-reliefs above the archways pay homage to the Empire's victories. The four bronze horses standing in state on the top of the arch are replicas of the ones that Napoleon had brought back from Italy and

The Tuileries Gardens.

52

The Venus de Milo, in the Louvre.

The Tuileries Gardens

Successive monarchs were at pains to improve the gardens. For Catherine de Medici, Jean Le Nôtre laid out an Italian-style park, a pleasant place for a stroll for the small group of courtiers. In the reign of Louis XIV, André Le Nôtre, the previous gardener's grandson, gave the park its Classical appearance and built the two terraces — des Feuillants and du Bord-de-l'Eau (the Terrasse des Feuillants was the site of the Manège in which the National Assembly met in 1789). At that time, the gardens were open to the public. In the 18th century people could even take their ease on hired chairs and watch the first experiments with hot air balloons. Coustou, Van Cleve and Coysevox have left us some magnificent statues.

The two pavilions that make up the Jeu de paume (or real tennis court, a sport which was very fashionable at that time and which was the forerunner of tennis as we know it today) were built in 1853. They are now used as art galleries.

Opposite is the Musée de l'Orangerie which houses some superb canvases by Claude Monet.

The Louvre Museum

Purchases, legacies, archaeological digs, royal patronage or military conquest have all gone to create the wealth and astonishing diversity of museum exhibits which have been put on show in a superb setting. The Venus de Milo, the Victory of Samothrace, the Mona Lisa (by da Vinci), « Death at Sardanaple » (by Delacroix), « Gilles » (by Watteau), the Avignon Pietà, the « Adoration » (by Georges de La Tour) are just some of the gems belonging to the museum.

that St. Mark's in Venice recovered in 1815. It was Bosio who sculpted the statue of Peace on the quadriga during the Restoration.

In the gardens, which were laid out in 1909, are Maillol's admirable sculptures, with their generous forms and gently-sloping outlines. The digs carried out in the Napoleon Courtyard and the Carrousel Gardens uncovered a whole urban district of days long gone which enjoyed its heyday in the 17th century. Among other features, experts found the workshop of Bernard de Palissy, a ceramic painter who was Catherine de Medici's protege (several thousand contemporary items were collected).

The efforts made since 1932 to improve the layout of the museum with the backing of the writer André Malraux, the art teacher René Huyghe and the archaeologist André Parrot, have now been extended and modified by the restructuring of the museum as a whole. Visitors enter it by the pyramid on the Napoleon Courtyard. The underground Napoleon hall (auditorium, bookshop, restaurant, temporary exhibition hall and post office) receives 15,000 to 20,000 visitors a day. From there, they head off in the three main directions of any visit i.e. the Sully, Richelieu and Denon Wings. Note the wonderful spiral staircase and the piston-operated lift.

There are three floors containing the exhibitions of oriental, Greek, Etruscan and Roman antiquities, Egyptian antiquities, objets d'art sculptures, and paintings. Of all the "new rooms", the ones dealing with the history of the Louvre are the most spectacular.

The museum also houses a few **temporary exhibitions** presenting sketches, engravings, water colours and pastels, none of which would be suitable for a permanent show, as well as the latest acquisitions and the « Files of the Paintings Section ».

The **Marsan Wing**, which was rebuilt during the Third Republic, contains the the **Museum of Arts and Fashion** and the highly « practical » **Museum of Decorative Arts** with 50,000 items retracing the artistic development of several civilisations at different periods and in various fields.

The « Joconde »

The Victory of Samothrace, in the Louvre (above).

The new area in the Louvre Museum (below).

The Madeleine.

THE MADELEINE CHURCH
(Madeleine metro station)

« A temple of Glory in honour of the Great Army » — such was the wish formulated by Napoleon in 1806 when building work started again on the **chapel** which had been started during the reign of Louis XV. However, when Louis XVIII mounted the throne, he took up the original plan dating from 1764 and had the building made into a church dedicated to St. Mary Magdalene. It was not to be completed until **1842**. From the outside, it resembles a **Greco-Roman temple**. The 52 Corinthian columns 65 ft. high are topped by a 33 ft. pediment on which Lemaire carved a scene from the Last Judgement. A flight of 28 steps leads beyond the bronze door to an interior that is unusual for a church—the single aisle stretches out beneath light from three domes. There are neither side aisles nor transept. The chancel is semicircular. The Church of Mary Magdalene has no belltower and no cross. Lying along a north-south axis, it opens onto the luxurious **rue Royale**, a shrine to haute cuisine. It is also worth taking a stroll through the flower market on the left-hand side of the church.

THE MARAIS DISTRICT
(Saint-Paul metro station)

The name Lutetia given to Paris during the Gallo-Roman period conjures up pictures of the numerous **marshes** that covered certain areas of the town around the Seine and which were not drained until the Middle Ages. In the 13th-century, a religious community began to develop, marked by the presence of the Order of the Knights Templar — the rue du Temple serves as a reminder of their existence. Philip Augustus had the district protected by a wall and Charles V chose the aint-Paul Residence (demoli-shed in the 16th-century) as the royal palace, bringing in his wake high-ranking dignitaries and no-ables who had aristocratic man-sions built around the **place Royale** (now the place des Vosges) that had been laid out in Henri IV 's day In the 18th-centu-ry, though, aristocrats and finan-ciers deserted the Marais for Saint-Germain or Saint-Honoré leaving their mansions to trades-men and craftsmen.

Demolition work in the l9th-century spared a few of the man-sions, which were restored and protected by government inter-vention in 1962 with a view to sa-feguarding places of historic in-terest.

The Carnavalet Museum in the Marais District.

"A joust beneath Notre-Dame Bridge", a painting by Jean-Baptiste Raguenet, in the Carnavalet Museum.

The Carnavalet Residence

It was built during the Renaissance for one of the Presidents of the Parliament, probably by Pierre Lescot and Jean Goujon. It was the name of the second owner, Mme de Kernevenoy, changed to «Carnavalet» which has remained attached to the property. In the 17th-century, Androuet du Cerceau and later François Mansart gave it its present appearance. From 1676 onwards, it accommodated the Marquise de Sévigné. Extended in 1866 by the Town Council who was by then its owner, it now houses a **museum** showing the various stages in the capital's history from Prehistoric times to the present day, based on objects retrieved during archaeological digs, works of art and items that once belonged to the mansion's owners.

The Sens Residence

It dates from the late Middle Ages and is a blend of Gothic and Renaissance architecture. Originally, it was the **residence of the Bishops of Sens** who had authority over the Parisian bishops. In 1605 Margaret of Valois, Queen Margot, who had been repudiated by Henry IV, settled in the mansion. Then the bishops put it up for rent. By the time restoration work began in the early years of this century, the mansion had already suffered badly. The **Forney Library** which it houses at present is devoted to decorative and fine arts, sciences and industrial technology.

The Soubise Residence

In 1705, the Prince de Rohan-Soubise had a mansion built on the site of the original 14th-century residence erected for the Constable of France, Olivier de Clisson. The architect Delamair was responsible for its design.

The **Gothic entrance** that can still be seen today came from the Clisson Residence. In 1730, **Boffrand** was commissioned to design the interior decoration. Assisted by Boucher, Natoire and Van Loo, he arranged lavish apartments for the Prince and Princess de Soubise.

Since 1808, the palace has housed the **National Archives** which came into being in 1789. A **Museum of French History** consists of a collection of authentic historic documents (including the Edict of Nantes presented amidst old works of art and sculptures in an 18th-century setting.

Opposite this residence, and during the same period, Delamair built the **Rohan-Strasburg Residence** for the Bishop of Strasburg, Cardinal and Grand Almoner of France.

Sully, a former minister to Henri IV, had Jean Androuet Du Cerceau design the residence which bears his name in 1634. Once it had been purchased by the State, the annexes that overcrowded it in the 18th-century were demolished, giving it back its original appearance.

The **Lamoignon Residence**, dating from the end of the 16th-century, belonged to Diana of France, the natural daughter of Henri II. In the 17th-century Lamoignon, the first President of the Parliament of Paris, received a number of illustrious visitors there — Racine, Boileau, Mme de Sévigné, and Regnard. The literary torch was taken up again a century later by the mansion's new occupant, Alphonse Daudet. Since 1969, the mansion has housed the **Historic Library of the City of Paris**.

The place des Vosges
(Saint-Paul or Chemin-Vert metro station)

The decision taken in 1965 to restore the square has given it back all its original magnificence.

The Place des Vosges.

It is a perfect square with sides 350 ft. long, whose arcades support 36 brick and stone houses with slate roofs in a harmonious blend of pink, white and grey. In the centre, the gardens surrounded by iron railings (dating from the 17th century) and two hundred-year-old trees are dominated by the **equestrian statue of Louis XIII** which, after having inevitably been melted down during the Revolution, was recast in 1825.

In the 15th-century the **Tournelles Residence** stood on this former piece of marshland but Catherine de Medici got rid of it after her husband had been killed there in a tournament. It was in 1607 that Henri IV ordered the construction of a perfectly-designed symmetrical square with no detached properties. He had two **pavilions** built opposite each other, the **King's** and the **Queen's**. Until the end of the 18th-century, the place Royale attracted the elegant upper classes who arranged parties—and duels. It took the name « place des Vosges » in 1800 in honor of the first county to pay all its taxes. Visitors may wish to linger at No. 1 *bis*, the former Coulanges Mansion where the Marquise de Sévigné was born in 1626, and at No. 6 where **Victor Hugo** lived—today it is a **museum** in which, through a variety of documents, manuscripts, letters, drawings or furniture carved by the poet himself, one can glean some idea of the less well-known aspects of his character. No. 11 keeps alive the memory of Marion Delorme, No. 17 that of Bossuet and No. 21 that of Richelieu.

The Ministry of Finance.

MINISTRY OF FINANCE
(Bercy metro station)

When, in September 1981, François Mitterand announced his intention of "returning the Louvre to the History of France", he also annouced the departure of the Ministry of Finance, which had been housed in the Richelieu Wing for 110 years.

Its transfer to **Bercy** in June 1989 had a twofold purpose - to mark the new development of eastern Paris, counterbalancing the Défense and Porte Maillot districts in the west, and to bring back under one roof many of the different Ministry departments, while providing the Ministry with a modern environment in which to function.

Five buildings were constructed on a site covering just over 12 acres, at a cost of one-and-a-half billion francs. The buildings provide 2,800,000 sq. ft. of office space for a staff of 6,000. Buildings A, B and C were designed by Huidobro and Chemetov, while the other two (the glass and steel D and E) were an additional project designed by Arretche and Karasinsky.

Designed "in the horizontal plane", like a sort of viaduct standing opposite the Paris-Bercy Sports Hall, the huge building is particularly noticeable for **Building A,** a crossbar 975 yds. long straddling the riverside roads, lying parallel to the Boulevard de Bercy and perpendicular to the Quai de la Rapée. It houses 4 ministries (or Secretary of States' Offices), and includes official accommodation, offices, conference rooms, reception rooms and a foyer.

In order to soften the austerity of its architecture and building materials, the Ministry also includes particularly ornate open spaces in and around the buildings (a moat, landscaped terraces, private walkways, and patios).

Offices and individual buildings are set out around the main courtyard, on a pile in the Seine, and above the Quai de la Rapée (designers : I. Hebey and A. Putman).

In addition, an experimental approach gave the architects an opportunity to provide the best possible layouts in the offices as regards furnishings, electricity supplies, lighting, acoustics and spatial flexibility.

The buildings in Bercy are "smart", i.e. they are precabled throughout. The various workstations can communicate with each other and with external data bases.

The Place du Tertre.

Finally, as part of the "1% for artistic creation" scheme, the new buildings include works by contemporary artists or loans from museums (paintings, sculptures, tapestries, mural mosaics, decorative benches etc.)

MONTMARTRE
(Abbesses or Anvers metro station)

This former suburban village, annexed comparatively recently to the city of Paris (du-

Flights of steps up to Montmartre.

tal. The large numbers of tourists who climb the steps or take the funicular railway to the top add yet more vividness to this district.

Mercury or St. Denis?

The etymology of the name has never been satisfactorily explained. Some believe it to come from « mons Mercuris », the **Mount of Mercury**, the Roman god of Trade and Travellers in whose honour an altar was built in the very first years of the Christian era. Others evoke the legend of the **Mount of Martyrs**, in memory of St. Denis, the first Bishop of Paris, and his companions Rustic and Eleuthere. They came to convert Roman and pagan Lutetia in the 3rd Century but were tortured in the town before being brought to the hill and beheaded. According to legend, St. Denis picked up his bloodstained head, stopped to wash it in the fountain that bears his name, and went on his way towards the spot on the hill named after him. This doubtless rather fanciful « Station of the Cross » nevertheless set its seal on the religious vocation of the village. St. Denis' sacrifice was not in vain since the Roman temples were replaced by a **church**. The forerunner of St. Peter's Chapel was used as a sanctuary for the **abbey** founded at the same time by the Benedictines whose Order was to remain on the hill until the Revolution. The convent contained a cemetery called the « **martyrium** », a place of pilgrimage which led to the founding of several religious orders — Carmel, Oratory, Visitation, and more importantly the Society of Jesus that was later to become the Jesuit Order, founded by Ignatius Loyola. At that time, Montmartre was a **rural community** with vineyards and windmills.

ring the reign of Napoleon III), is a blend of almost rural districts where there are still traces of the old vineyards and areas where the nightlife is often very colourful.

The profusion of artistic expression and a past history of independance explained in part by the unusual geographical situation (it lies at an altitude of 423 ft.) make the hill a favoured part of the capi-

A historic period of resistance

It was Henri IV who first troubled the peace of Montmartre during the **Siege of Paris in 1590**. The bell seemed to have tolled for the abbey which suffered badly and lost the support of the Parisian people. However, the discovery in 1611 of a tomb said to be that of St. Denis renewed interest in the convent and it was extended down the hill » by the building of a new convent on what we now now as the place des Abbesses. The « Ladies of Montmartre » stayed there until their Order died out in 1794 when Mme de Montmorency-Laval, the last of the 46 abbesses, went to the guillotine. In 1871, a series of bloody events occurred on the hill. The people of Montmartre revolted against the authority that had capitulated to the Prussians. The rebellion against the regular government forces during Thiers' presidency lasted for two months. Two years later, the National Assembly decided to launch the building of the **Sacré-Cœur**. The project answered a vow taken by a nun in Paray-le-Monial to whom Christ had appeared in the 17th century asking that a church be built dedicated to the Sacred Heart. The decision, though, coming as it did after the terrible defeats suffered at the hands of the Prussians, was also a way of preventing the spread of ideas developed by anti-clerical elements in society. The Sacré-Cœur was a symbolical appeal « for divine protection and goodness for France ».

The Muse of the Gay Nineties

The 19th-century also saw the **artistic heyday** of a Montmartre that had remained rustic and picturesque, far removed from the problems of Paris. It was an oasis of freedom and Bohemian life and even of starvation for the artists who lived only for Art although they did not as yet live off their artistry. On the place Émile-Goudeau, in the **Bateau-**

The Place du Tertre.

Lavoir that was burnt down in 1970, numerous painters developed their talents —Picasso, Van Dongen the forerunner of Fauvism, Braque the promoter of Cubism, Derain, Matisse, Degas, Poulbot, Suzanne Valadon and her son Utrillo, Modigliani, and the Impressionists Van Gogh and Corot. The old wooden building, the « poets' residence, » also housed Reverdy, Mac Orlan, Apollinaire, and Max Jacob who had the idea of the nickname (Bateau-Lavoir means « Laundry-Ship ») because of the linen hanging out the windows, as well as the American Gertrude Stein, Dorgelès, Charles Dullin who was responsible for the success of the Théâtre de l'Atelier, and Paul Doumer in the days before he became President of the Republic.

The « **Lapin Agile** », a bar in the rue des Saules, conjures up memories of the painter André Gill who made sketches of the tavern in 1880, the writer Francis Carco and the songwriter Aristide Bruant who launched the fashion for satirical realism. Nightlife spreads down to the place Blanche, to the « **Moulin Rouge** » which was a mere dancehall when it was opened in 1889. It was there that the French cancan was created under the watchful eye of Valentin le Désossé (the Boneless Man), la Goulue (the Glutton), Nini Patte-en-l'Air (Knees-up Nini), and le Pétomane (the Windbreaker), much to the delight of the Parisians of the Gay Nineties and the rich tourists. Offenbach found ideas for his operettas there and **Toulouse-Lautrec** fixed memories of wild celebrations and their ephemeral stars for all time on his posters. Another dancehall also attracted night owls — the « **Moulin de la Galette** » which provided Renoir with inspiration for his famous painting. The artist lived only a short distance away in a white house in the **allée des Brouillards**

The Moulin Roug

The Sacré Coeur Basilica.

where the **castle**, an 18th-century folly, was occupied in 1846 by the poet Gérard de Nerval.

The return of the picturesque

It would be easy to describe pellmell taverns like the « Chat Noir » (Black Cat) or « Bonne Franquette » (No standing on ceremony), the population of minor tradesmen like the ragmerchants and secondhand dealers, the wine drunk as people waited for « Cherry Time » or the « Delights of Love ». But artistic and literary enthusiasm waned when the First World War dawned. It was to come alive again in Montparnasse, leaving to Montmartre the mercantile night entertainments, a veritable pleasure industry which, from Pigalle to Rochechouart, has nothing to do with nostalgia. On the **place du Tertre**, the former village square, among the last vestiges of 18th-century buildings (including the town hall at No. 3) and amidst the taverns and restaurants besieged by visitors, would be artists and caricaturists try to re-create the old magic of Montmartre.

St. Peter's Church

This was the chapel for the Benedictines from the abbey « uphill ». Consecrated by the Pope Eugene III, in the 12th century, it is now one of the oldest churches in Paris. It still bears traces of Romanesque architecture. During restoration work in the 15th century, vaulting was built in place of the old wooden ceiling. The 18th century restoration concerned the West Front. In the early years of this century, the church was saved from the dilapidation that had set in during the Revolution (when it became a Temple of Reason) and had been worsened by the Russian occupation of 1814.

The Sacré-Cœur

Work began after the National Assembly had given it the go-ahead in **1876**. **Abadie**, who was in charge of the work, came up against the first problems when the foundations were dug. The loose soil had to be consolidated by wells 124 ft. deep. A subscription was launched on a nationwide basis and chapels pay homage to the assistance given by major bodies such as the Navy, the Army, the Medical Profession and the Fine Arts. The building work took almost forty years to complete, no notice being taken of the bitter disagreements it aroused. The basilica has managed to make people accept its extravagant architecture and today it stands high above the Paris landscape with its tall luminous white towers, its high dome, and its square belltower measuring 270 ft. housing one of the largest bells in existence, the « **Savoyarde** ». It weighs 19 metric tonnes and has a 850 kg. clapper. It was a gift from the clergy of Savoie at the end of the 19th-century. Although oriental in appearance, the church shows rather more a taste for imitation, with its blend of Romanesque and Byzantine architecture, than for any true religious inspiration. The magnificent bronze doors were

The Orsay Art Gallery.

the work of Hippolyte Lefèvre. The mosaics and statues inside are of only limited interest. Nevertheless, the solid silver statue of the Sacred Heart is worthy of note, as is the statue of St. Genevieve who is to be seen in many of the capital's churches as she is the patron saint of Paris. The treasure is hidden in the crypt.

Visitors emerging onto the **square Willette** will discover the superb and vast panorama of a Paris which has not always been looked upon with favour from up here.

In the **Montmartre cemetery** in the rue Caulaincourt are the graves of many well-known people —Fragonard, Greuze, Ampère, Stendhal, Vigny, Mme Récamier, Théophile Gautier, Léo Delibes, Offenbach, Degas, Poulbot, Alexandre Dumas the Younger, Berlioz, Heine, the Goncourt Brothers, Labiche, Giraudoux, Charcot, Louis Jouvet, Sacha Guitry and his father, etc.

ORSAY ART GALLERY
(Musée d'Orsay R.E.R. station)

It was the firm of A.C.T Architecture (Bardon, Colboc and Philippon) which picked up the challenge in the late 1980's viz. how to take the old Orsay Station, which had been built at the end of the 19th century by Victor Laloux (who also built the covered market designed by Baltard, the Halles) and been out of use since 1939 because it had become too cramped and turn what had been a listed building since 1978 into a **Modern Art Gallery** specialising entirely in art work from the second half of the **19th century** and the early years of the 20th (1848-1914).

In 1986, the first visitors stepped into a gigantic hall, the old station foyer, which Gae Aulenti, an Italian interior designer, had faced with golden-toned limestone. To each side of this central passage are marble and bronze sculptures (note the original plaster-cast of Jean-Baptiste Carpeaux' "The 4 parts of the world supporting the celestial sphere" dating from 1867-1872). The bas-relief known as "The Dance" (1869), also by Carpeaux, was still decorating the front of the Opera House only a few short years ago.

The Gallery's **collections** come from the **Louvre**, the Musée du Jeu de Paume, and the Palais de Tokyo (there was no room for them in the Pompidou Centre which opened in 1976). In addition, the

The Orsay Art Gallery.

Gallery has acquired legacies and donations.

The Gallery includes a wide variety of works, calling upon differing artistic techniques e.g. paintings, pastels, sculptures, photographs, *objets d'art*, architecture (designs and models), all of them very closely linked to the history of literature and music and all of them presented through thematic exhibitions, talks and concerts.

In addition to the sculptures mentioned above, the ground floor houses paintings. The ones to the right are eclectic and academic; the ones to the left were created by independent movements, Realists, landscape artists or Pre-Impressionists.

A staircase leads to the rooms housing the **Impressionists** and Post-Impressionists (Van Gogh,

Seurat, Gauguin etc.). Note, too, works by the Nabis (Bonnard, Vuillard, Valloton), Théodore Rousseau, and the Pont-Aven School. From the café, there is a wonderful view across the R.Seine.

In the domed rooms overlooking the Seine on the intermediate floor, are the official painters of the Third Republic, foreign schools and the Symbolists, Rodin, international Art Nouveau and an exhibition describing the birth of the cinema industry.

Also on this floor are the thematic exhibitions using a full range of disciplines to illustrate their subject matter or event.

Last but not least, do not miss the restaurant and the ballroom in the former station hotel.

On your way back downstairs, stop at the book and card shop on the ground floor before going out onto the Bellechasse Esplanade (reception area) where you can see the bronzes cast for the World Fair of 1878. Overlooking the riverside roadway are statues representing Bordeaux, Toulouse and Nantes by Hugues, Marqueste and Injalbert.

NOTRE-DAME
(*Cité metro station*)

Culturally-speaking, this is a place steeped in tradition. As far back as the 1st Century B.C. there was a Roman temple in honour of Jupiter on the site, replaced in the 6th century by the first Christian church in Paris built by Childebert, Clovis' son.

Maurice de Sully, the capital's bishop in the 12th century, had the idea of building a magnificent cathedral on the ruins of the previous religious buildings. He received donations from the clergy, the monarchy, the aristocracy and even from the poorer members of society who also provided him with his labour force. The work was directed from **1163** onwards by a first group of unknown architects, who completed the chancel, aisles and façade in 75 years. Jean de Chelles and Pierre de Montreuil (who also gave us the Sainte-Chapelle) organised the second part of the work, concerned mainly with the chapels, roodscreen, and façades of the transept and apse. It was finished by 1345.

At the same time, Notre-Dame was paid political and religious homage. In 1329, St. Louis came barefoot to place the Holy Relics in it; they were later transferred to the Sainte-Chapelle. The King's body was brought back from Tunis where he had died of the Black Death and final tributes were paid in the cathedral in 1270. On the eve of the first States General in 1302, Philip the Fair came here to seek the protection of the Virgin Mary. King Henry VI of England was crowned King of France in 1430 and, in 1594, the Protestant Henri

Van Gogh, the Orsay Art Gallery.

The chevet of Notre-Dame.

The West Front of Notre-Dame de Paris.

IV who had decided that « Paris is worth going to Mass for » was converted to Catholicism. It was also in Notre-Dame that Louis XIV was married in 1660 and that Condé's funeral was held in 1687, when Bossuet gave the funeral oration.

The building began to fall into disrepair as far back as the 17th century when Louis XIV, respecting a vow made by his father, ordered a disastrous redecoration project. During it, the superb 12th-century windows decorating the nave were replaced by white glass, the walls were painted, the rood-screen was demolished, and some of the carvings on the façade were destroyed. A few years later, revolutionaries attacked the statues of the Kings of Judah which they thought represented the Kings of France. Damage ceased when Robespierre decreed that the goddess Reason should be worshipped in a cathedral that had been made into a temple. It was not returned to the Catholic church until 1802 and was still licking its wounds when Napoleon I was crowned there by Pope Pius VII two years later. It was, though, the publishing of Victor Hugo's book, « The Hunchback of Notre-Dame », in 1831 which refired people's interest in the monument and led to sufficient government grants to permit its restoration. The project was the work of Viollet-le-Duc. He spent more than twenty years on it (until 1864), doing his utmost to respect the original 14th-century spirit. In 1870, Notre-Dame escaped destruction — it also remained intact after the bombing of 1944. In 1970, a Requiem Mass was held there in memory of General de Gaulle.

THE OUTSIDE

From the huge parvis which Haussmann increased fourfold last century, there is a good view of the soaring Gothic façade. Pillars divide it into three vertical axes cut horizontally by galleries, giving the building its perfect balance and sumptuous airiness.

The "Coronation of the Virgin Mary" tympanum.

The south side of the cathedral (on previous pages).

As so often in mediaeval buildings, the three entrances are all different. The central doorway is larger than the other two, and the one on the left is noticeable for its gable. All of them have superb doors decorated with wrought-iron work. Most of the carvings date from the 13th century but in some instances they were rebuilt during the 19th century restoration. In general, they are a reminder of the pictorial art so beloved of mediaeval sculptors.

In the centre of the **Virgin Mary Portal** on the left is a modern copy of the statue of the Madonna and Child. The tympanum has carvings of Death, and the Coronation and Assumption of Mary who is shown enthroned amidst prophets and kings. The bas-reliefs on each side of the doors represent seasonal work although the rhythm is broken up by signs of the zodiac.

In the centre, on the **Last Judgement Portal** that was altered in the 18th century but restored by Viollet-le-Duc, Christ (on the tympanum) is flanked by the Virgin Mary and St. John bearing the symbols of His Passion and is presiding over the ceremonies of the Resurrection (on the bottom) and the weighing of souls (in the centre). Abraham welcomes to Paradise those who have been saved (on the left) while the others join the demons in Hell (on the right). In the 19th century, allegories of the Vices and Virtues and statues of the Twelves Apostles were added to each side of the statue of Christ on the central pillar.

The right-hand doorway, or **St. Anne's Portal**, bears the oldest carvings in the cathedral (1170). The Virgin Mary, to whom the church is dedicated, is shown with the Child Jesus, two angels, Bishop Maurice de Sully and Louis VII, and with her parents St. Anne and St. Joachim. On the pillar in the centre St. Marcel, the town's bi-

The west rose window seen from the outside.

shop in the 5th century, is shown fighting a dragon. The original statue is kept in the North Tower.

Above the portals, the **Kings' Gallery** again bears the statues of the Kings of Judah and Israel that were damaged during the Revolution and redesigned by Viollet-le-Duc.

The twin windows in the upper section add to the brilliance of the 13th-century **rose window** 33 ft. in diameter, which still has its original stained glass. The statues of Adam (on the left), the Madonna and Child flanked by two angels, and Eve (on the right) provide the decoration on this level.

At the foot of the towers is a row of **arcading** on which Viollet-le-Duc created a whole fantasy world of monsters, witches and devils.

The unfinished towers have no steeples but they nevertheless give the building an overall height of 227 ft. They each contain two deep-set windows that are more than 52 ft. long. It is the South Tower that houses the 13-tonne bell whose 1,100 lb. clapper, which was recast during the reign of Louis XIV (using women's jewellery according to tradition), is now worked by electricity.

On the north side of Notre-Dame is the 13th-century **Cloisters Portal** through which the canons used to enter the cathedral. The two rows of carvings retell the story of Deacon Théophile whom the Virgin Mary prevented from making a pact with the Devil.

The **Red Door** a little further on, built by Pierre de Montreuil illustrates the Coronation of the Virgin Mary and the life of St Marcel.

On the other side of the cathedral is the apse with its wonderful 50-foot **flying buttresses** (built by Jean Ravy in the 14th century) which seem to be such an integral part of the cathedral that their architectural rôle is forgotten.

The **steeple** is the work of Viollet-le-Duc. It is 146 ft. high (its tip stands 292 ft. above the ground) and its 750 tonnes are a blend of lead and oak.

One of Notre-Dame's gargoyles.

The nave.

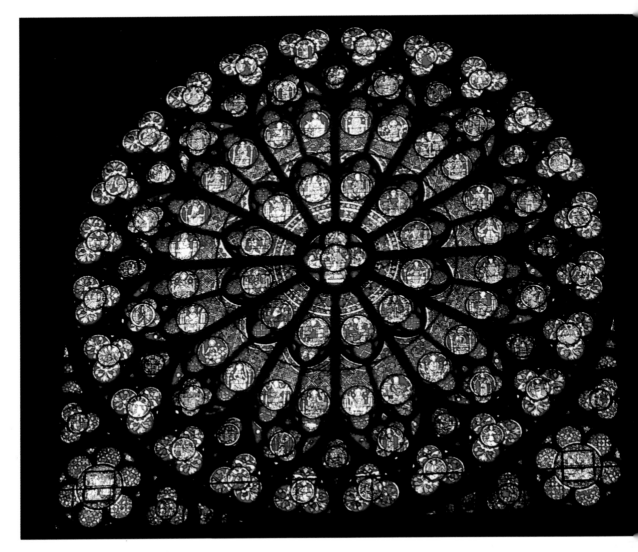

The rose window in the south transept.

Finally, opposite the Cloisters Portal is **St. Stephen's Portal**, designed by Jean de Chelles and Pierre de Montreuil. It is dedicated to the saint whose name it bears and also depicts scenes from student life in the 13th century.

THE INTERIOR

The cathedral is a majestic 420 ft. long, 162 ft. wide, and 114 ft. high. It can hold as many as 9,000 people, including 1,500 in the galleries.

The 29 chapels dating from the 13th and 14th centuries are decorated with 17th-century paintings, gifts from the gold-smiths to mark the 1st May every year. The chapels flank a 12th-century nave, subtly lit by modern stained glass windows (made by Le Chevalier in the 60's) based on the mediaeval originals. Cliquot's organ, which was built in the 18th century and restored in the 19th, is the largest in France with its 6,000 pipe and 113 stops.

The stained glass and ros windows in the transept provide whole gamut of softly-coloure lights. The North rose window which has suffered little damag since it was made in 1250, ren ders homage around the magnifi cent blue-tinted Virgin Mary t people from the Old Testament The South rose window suffere restoration in the 18th-century. depicts Christ surrounded by vir gins and saints.

At the entrance to the chancel, Nicolas Coysevox sculpted a statue of St. Denis in the 18th-century. The Virgin and Child (or « Our Lady of Paris ») dates from the 14th-century. The chancel contains some very fine 18th-century choir stalls, and is decorated with a Pietà by Nicolas Coustou (1723) flanked by statues of a kneeling Louis XIII (by Guillaume Coustou in 1715) and Louis XIV (by Coysevox in the same period).

The 14th-century wrought-iron grille was restored in the 19th-century. In the crypt underneath the chancel are the graves of the former Bishops of Paris.

The sacristy built by Viollet-le-Duc houses the cathedral treasure whose relics and various exhibits attest to the glorious 800-hundred-year history of Notre-Dame.

THE OBSERVATORY
(Saint-Jacques metro station)

The Luxembourg Gardens open onto the flowerbeds in the avenue de l'Observatoire laid out by Chalgrin on the site of the former Carthusian monastery. From amidst the greenery springs the **fountain** designed by Davioud in 1873. Frémiet carved the **Sea-horses** and Carpeaux the famous allegories of the four areas of the world cast in bronze.

It was Colbert who ordered Claude Perrault to begin work on an Observatory in 1667. Its four walls are in line with the four points of the compass. The experiments carried out here over the past three centuries have led to major progress in the field of astronomy. Today, the Observatory is the headquarters of the International Time Office where world times are coordinated. It also houses the speaking clock and a museum.

THE OPERA HOUSE
(Opéra metro station)

It was the design submitted by **Charles Garnier**, a young architect aged just 35, which was chosen from among the 171 presented prior to the building of an opera house. Building work on this « Napoleon III-style » palace got underway in **1862**. The water-logged subsoil, though, had to be drained, and the damage caused by fire in 1873 had to be repaired. The inauguration finally took place in 1875, in the presence of Mac-Mahon, the recently elected President of the Republic. The

The fountain in the Observatory.

largest lyric theater in the world covers an area of 11,000 sq. m. The auditorium can seat 2,200 people in the stalls and four balconies. The stage is 169 ft. wide, 215 ft. high, and 120 ft. deep, and it can hold 450 actors or members of cast. The gigantic chandelier, which in fact collapsed one evening in 1896, weighs 6 metric tonnes and carries 400 light bulbs.

The **main façade** overlooks the place de l'Opéra. A permanently-lit attic tops the arches decorated with a multiplicity of statues. The most famous sculpture is the one by Carpeaux called « The Dance, » of which visitors see a replica made in 1964 by Paul Belmondo (the original, threatened by weathering, is kept in the Orsay Museum). On the sides are busts of musicians. The West Wing, which was originally intended for the Emperor's use, now houses the museum and library.

The **museum** contains various pieces of memorabilia, busts, models and paintings showing the former opera house in the rue Le Pelletier, which was destroyed by fire in 1871. The **library** contains 80,000 volumes retracing the musical, theatrical and choreo graphic history of the opera house, with all the musical scores used since 1669.

The **great staircase** has marble steps 32 ft. wide; the bannister is made of Algerian onyx. The great foyer (176 ft. long, 43 ft. wide, and 39 ft. high) is decorated with busts and paintings. The Imperial-style auditorium has, since 1964, been the proud owner of a new removable ceiling for which **Chagall** sought inspiration in famous operas.

The Paris Opera House.

BASTILLE OPERA HOUSE
(Bastille metro station)

The site once occupied by a railway station and, even further back in time, by the highly symbolic fortress of 1789, has been the setting since July 1989 of the Bastille Opera House, a modern functional theatre designed to bring a new ("popular") audience into contact with the lyric art.

It was a young Canadian architect of Uruguayan origin, Carlos Ott, who, in 1983, won the competition that had been launched one year earlier. Building work began in November 1984. After four years of work at a cost of 2.17 billion francs, the simple geometrical construction (half-cylinders, parallelepipeds, and porticoes) underlined by its transparency (on the main facade) and the sense of openness (there are numerous entrances and exits) rests on 37 acres of flooring and has a height of 156 ft.

The **main auditorium**, which is built of bluish granite, is the largest lyric theatre in France. It has 2,700 pearwood seats covered in black velvet and is designed to cater for three times as many people as in a traditional opera audience, in optimum conditions as regards visibility and acoustics, whether the performance is one of the great classics or a contemporary work.

Below it is a 600-seat **amphitheatre**, a basement theatre suitable for a wide variety of entertainments (concerts, recitals, films, exhibitions etc.).

The **Silver Tower Studio** (280 seats) is, as its name suggests, on the upper floor of the adjacent restaurant (Restaurant de la Tour d'Argent).

Provision has also been made for a modular auditorium seating between 600 and 1,000.

The advantages of the Bastille Opera House compared to the Opéra Garnier are the flexibility of its equipment, and its alternating and repetitive spaces. The Bastille Opera, the first opera house to be built in Paris for one hundred years, was to house up to six different performances per week. To date, only one concert has been staged there (Bob Wilson, "La nuit avant le Jour"), for the inauguration. The Opera has had a succession of musical directors, for reasons that usually have little to do with music. The latest one is a Korean, Myung Whun Chung, which augurs well for the international development of this operatic establishment.

The Bastille Opera House.

The Trocadéro Gardens.

THE PALAIS DE CHAILLOT
(Trocadéro metro station)

The Chaillot Hill was chosen by Catherine de Medici in the 16th century as the site of a house that later became a convent. In the early 19th-century, Napoleon planned to have a palace built there for his son, the King of Rome, and directed Percier and Fontaine to take charge of the work. It came to a halt with the downfall of the Empire. It was not until 1878, the year of the World Fair, that the first Chaillot Palace was built. It was of Spanish inspiration and was called Trocadéro after a campaign during the Spanish War in 1823. The palace was modernised for the 1937 World Fair by the architects Carlu, Boileau, and Azéma who kept the two 228 ft. minarets towering over the 196 ft. terrace with the theatre underneath. The two 634 ft. long semi-circular **wings** beyond the two huge **pavilions** are covered with a gilded limestone cladding. The gilded inscriptions on the pediments are by Paul Valéry. These days, the wings house a number of **museums** — the Museum of Man and the Navy Museum, the Museum of French Monuments (which has a collection of very fine architectural moulds and models), the Film Museum, and a film library.

The **Chaillot National Theatre** reached its glorious heyday in the time of Jean Vilar who directed the « National Theatre of the People » (the

The Palais de Chaillot.

« T.N.P. ») until 1963 with assistance from Gérard Philippe. Now the auditorium can be adapted for various types of show thanks to its modern layout. It can seat up to 1,800 people. Another auditorium, the Gémier Theatre, was built in 1966 for more « intimate » drama.

The Palais de Chaillot boasts a number of superb sculptures and bas-reliefs. Bou-chard created the huge gilded bronze statues towering above the terrace. An equestrian statue was erected on the **place du Trocadéro-et-du-11-novembre** in honour of Maréchal Foch who signed the Armistice in 1918.

Gardens ornamented with fountains and aquariums stretch down to the Seine in a series of terraces.

The watercannon in action.

LAW COURTS
Palais de Justice
(Cité metro station)
Ile de la Cité

As far back as the 3rd Century B.C. the Parisii, who were mainly Seine boatmen, lived « in the midst of the waters » in the town of Lutetia where Caesar installed his first Roman legions in 52 B.C. During the Gallo-Roman period, the « city » (or « civitas ») organised itself into a municipality. Governors and emperors settled in a palace which was attacked from the 5th century A.D. onwards by Barbarian, Merovingian and Capetian invaders. The town took advantage of this and expanded onto the left bank of the river. Louis VI and Louis VII inherited the royal palace which St. Louis and Philip the Fair later extended. When, in the 14th century, the kings left it in favour of the Louvre or the Saint-Paul Mansion, it became the seat of the Parliament, the highest court of justice in the land originally presided over by specialists nominated by the monarch. In the 16th century, it became a purchasable then a hereditary office. It was the Parliament which was to summon the States General, involuntarily paving the way for the Revolution. A new legal institution came into being after 1789, making the former royal residence and Parliament a Court of Law.

The gilded gates of the Law Courts.

Restoration work was undertaken in 1840 and was completed just before the outbreak of the First World War. In the meantime, a fire lit during the riots of the Commune meant that the west front overlooking the place Dauphine had to be rebuilt.

A wrought-iron grille, a very fine place of craftsmanship dating from the 18th century, leads into the **Maypole Courtyard** which was decorated with a new tree

The Luxembourg Gardens.

brought by the clerks on the first day of that particular month every year. The Louis XVI **Great Staircase** takes visitors up to the **lobby** and the **Gilded Chamber**, now the first Civil Court. As a High Chamber, it was probably occupied by St. Louis. The Parliament turned it into its Great Chamber, and Fouquier-Tinville made it the seat of the Revolutionary Tribunal. Both chambers underwent restoration work in the 19th century.

The Law Courts are part and parcel of the Conciergerie and

Sainte-Chapelle but are not open to the public.

THE PALAIS DU LUXEMBOURG
(Luxembourg R.E.R. station)

The Luxembourg proudly bears traces of History and Art — it was placed under their dual sign from the outset when it was built in the 17th century. In 1612 **Marie de Medici,** with longings for her home, the Pitti Palace in Florence,

87

bought a **mansion** and park from the Duc de Luxembourg. Salomon de Brosse was ordered to design the new royal residence and the Queen moved here from the Louvre in 1625. Rubens then began a series of 24 paintings retracing the life of the sovereign (they are now kept in the Louvre). Philippe de Champaigne and Nicolas Poussin also did some of the decoration. In order to ingratiate herself with Richelieu, the Queen made him a present of the **Petit Luxembourg**. However, the completion of the building work in 1630 coincided with her own downfall and she was forced into exile in Cologne. The royal family retained the property rights to the Luxembourg which then became the centre of a literary and artistic world (a museum and a literary academy were opened there). With the Revolution, the palace became a prison. When Bonaparte became Consul, he had the outside altered by Chalgrin and a debating chamber installed for the newly-constituted **Senate**. In the 19th-century, the extension of the Assembly brought other alterations carried out in the main by Gisors. During the Paris Commune, the Senate was transferred to Versailles, and the Palais du Luxembourg became an annex of the Val-de-Grâce hospital. The museum had, at that time, a very well-known curator — none other than the painter, Courbet. Since 1879, the Senate has sat in the Luxembourg and the President's official residence has been the Petit Luxembourg comprising the former Richelieu Mansion, the cloisters and the chapel.

The bosses in the palace, the ringed pillars and the capitals are all of Florentine inspiration, but the façade and two wings were typical-

The Palais du Luxembourg.

ly French. In the former **library** are paintings by Delacroix (1847) and, on the ceiling of a nearby gallery, are the signs of the zodiac by the Flemish painter Joardens. The **great staircase** was designed by Chalgrin.

The **gardens**, standing on the site of the 13th-century Carthusian monastery (built after the monks had exorcised the famous devil who haunted the place), are a veritable haven of peace and tranquillity amidst the hubbub of the Latin Quarter. They underwent major alteration in the early 19th century (under the aegis of Chalgrin) and again in the Second Empire, and are a hesitant blend of a cottage-style English garden with winding paths and the formal staggered layout of French parks. The **Medici Fountain** is said to have been designed by Salomon de Brosse. The bas-relief of « Leda and her swan » (1807) was the work of Chalgrin. Ottin carved the statue of Polyphemus in 1863—the cyclops is about to crush to death the Sicilian shepherd Acis who preferred the goddess Galatea. Dalou sculpted the memorial to Delacroix. The statues, which were placed in the gardens in the reign of Louis-Philippe, are now almost as numerous as the students who crowded along its pathways. A **puppet theatre** gives several performances a day, to the great delight of the children who are particularly fond of the park.

THE PALAIS-ROYAL
(Palais-Royal metro station)

The Palais-Royal, its galleries, gardens and the Comédie-Française are a haven of peace in the heart of Paris, breaking with years of intense tumultuous activity.

In 1632, Le Mercier began the building opposite the Louvre of a palace for Cardinal Richelieu who, on his death in 1642, left it to Louis XIII. The Regent, Anne of Austria, took up residence with her son, the future Louis XIV, in the « **Palais-Cardinal** » which was then renamed the Palais-Royal. She lived in style until the uprisings of the Fronde. Louis XIV mounted the throne, settled in the Louvre, and lodged his

The Buren Columns in the Palais-Royal.

istress, Mlle de La Vallière, in the alace before giving it to his bro- ner. It then became the property of ne Orléans family. The first Duc 'Orléans had alterations carried ut and gave splendid supper par- es and lavish balls there. This was ne time when the palace could take ride in the prestigious collection of aintings from all over the world.

In 1780, Louis-Philippe d'Or- éans had gaming houses built round the park as well as glass **hopping arcades**, thereby attrac- ng crowds of people who also ook advantage of the cafés, restau- nts, literary taverns or shops spe- ialising in fancy goods. The Palais- Royal, which was State property uring the Revolution, became a opular debating chamber before eing called « **Palais-Égalité** » vith the return of the Orléans fami- y to the throne. It was little more han a gambling den when Napo- eon decided to instal the govern- nent offices, stock exchange and rade Court there. It was ransacked nd burned during the riots in 1848 nd again during the Commune. rom 1872 to 1876, Chabrol did his tmost to restore it. Today, it is the eat of the **Council of State**.

Set up in 1985-86 in the main ourtyard that opens onto the gar- lens, the **columns** of varying eights designed by **Daniel Buren** ave been the subject of some ontroversy. They are decorated vith grey and white stripes and are et out in a checkerboard pattern on concrete base crisscrossed by mat- hing lines.

Pol Bury's **sculptures** (1985), vhich decorate the fountains in the allery, form moving clusters of teel that reflect the buildings round bout.

he Palais-Royal (top).

he Panthéon (bottom).

THE PANTHEON
(Luxembourg R.E.R. station)

The crypt of the Panthéon, the « lay and republican Saint-Denis, » contains the mortal remains of civilian personalities and is a sort of mirror image of the military graves in the Arc de Triomphe and Invalides. The Conventional Lazare Carnot and his son Sadi, the author Zola, the M.P. Baudin, the chemist Berthelot and his wife, Louis Braille, Paul Painlevé, the politician Jean Jaurès, the physicians Jean Perrin and Paul Langevin, the Resistance leader Jean Moulin, and heroes of the Revolution and the Empire were all buried here. It was during the days of the Constituant Assembly that the following words were carved on the pediment, « To great men from a grateful country ».

Yet at the outset, the building was to serve a religious purpose. In answer to a vow made during a serious illness, Louis XV ordered the building of a superb church on the site of an ancient chapel dedicated to St. Genevieve, patron saint of Paris. Soufflot began work in 1755 but it was to be a slow and costly business (the king had to resort to lotteries to raise funds). Rondelet completed the gigantic monument after 1780 — it measures 358 ft. by 273 ft. and is 267 ft. high. The Revolution, which made it into a pantheon, paid homage to less religious gods. The bay windows and side doors were walled up, two towers were knocked down and the crosses were removed. Mirabeau, Voltaire, and Rousseau were buried there. The building was given back to the church during Napo-

The Panthéon.

The Place des Victoires.

The Panthéon (opposite).

leon's reign, was again turned into a pantheon under Louis-Philippe, and became a place of worship during Napoleon III 's day. When it received Victor Hugo's ashes in 1885, it became a civil monument once and for all. These numerous changes of use had a considerable effect on the building.

The antique façade with its Corinthian columns is topped by a **pediment** decorated with a sculpture by David (1831) setting out the relationship between « Country, Liberty, and History ». The interior has the shape of a Greek cross. Beneath the dome, a fresco by Gros (1811) illustrates the « Apotheosis of St. Genevieve » whose story Puvis de Chavannes retold in the left-hand side of the chancel while Laurens illustrated her death on the right-hand side. There are also a few admirable 19th and 20th-century sculptures.

The **dome** has 32 columns of the same architectural order as those on the façade, and is reminiscent of St. Paul's Cathedral in London. It still has the stone cross which was erected in 1873.

PLACE DES VICTOIRES
(Bourse metro station)

The Duc de Feuillade, one of Louis XIV 's courtiers who wanted to pay homage to his sovereign, ordered a marble statue of the king from the sculptor Desjardins. In order to give the monument surroundings worthy of it, he had plans for an oval square drawn up by Jules Hardouin-Mansart — its mansions, all built in the same style, form a superb harmonious setting. The statue of the Sun King was demolished in 1792 while the ones that flanked it went to the Public Gardens in Sceaux and the bas-reliefs were placed in the Louvre. A new statue was erected by Bosio in 1822. The tradesmen who began to swarm here from the l9th century onwards inflicted serious damage on the square and its balance was upset once and for all in 1833 with the laying out of the rue Etienne-Marcel. The very fine arcaded mansions provided accommodation for a number of illustrious people including the financiers Crozat and Samuel Bernard.

THE PLACE VENDÔME
(Pyramides-Opéra metro station)

Jules Hardouin-Mansart designed and built this **Royal Square** which was originally dedicated like the place des Victoires, to Louis XIV. It was built between 1687 and 1720, on the site of the mansion belonging to the Duke of Vendôme, the son of Henri IV and Gabrielle d'Estrées. The equestrian statue of Louis XIV, erected in 1699 by Girardon, was destroyed during the Revolution. The square was to house the monarchy's administrative offices and institutions but the land behind the superb façades became the subject of property speculation and was bought up by bankers, Farmers General (one of whom was Law), and architects (including Hardouin-Mansart and Boffrand). The octagon measuring 242 yds. by 231 yds. then became a very fine piece of architecture — on the ground floor were arcades alternating with fore-parts, while skylights are set in the roofs right at the top. The **mansions** round the edge of the square have accommodated several V.I.P.'s in the days of the monarchy, and during the Revolution Chopin died at No. 12. The prestigious Ritz is at No. 19. The Ministry of Justice occupies Nos. 11 and 13 (previously the Chancellory of the kingdom). Jewellers, perfumeries, and bankers attract a very high class clientèle to the square.

The **column** was built in 1810 during the reign of Napoleon I, to replace the equestrian statue of Louis XIV. Standing 143 ft. high and based on Trajan's Column in Rome, it was cast using the 12,000 cannon brought back from Austerlitz in honour of the exploits of Napoleon's armies. In 1814, Napoleon's statue was replaced in its turn by one of Henri IV, then, in 1833 (during the reign of Louis

The Place Vendôme.

The Pont-Neuf (above and overleaf).

Philippe), by a statue of the empe-ror dressed as the Little Corporal. The monument was again unbolted from its base during the Paris Commune—notably at the instiga-ion of the painter, Courbet. A eplica of the original statue repre-senting Napoleon dressed as a Ro-nan Emperor was erected in 1874, at the painter's expense.

THE PONT-NEUF
(Pont-Neuf metro station)

Despite its name, this is the ol-lest bridge in Paris. It has kept its original shape (hence the popular French expression « se porter com-me le Pont-Neuf » or « to wear as well as the Pont-Neuf »). Du Cer-ceau began it in **1578** and Henri IV inaugurated it on horseback on 1607. It connected the western pro-montory of the Ile de la Cité to the two small islets called Jews' Island and Patriarch's Island and was a fore-runner of the future quays. Its desi-gn was something quite new. It was a very wide bridge where pedes-trians walked along **pavements** from which they could see the Seine since the view was not obstructed by any houses. It quickly became a meeting-place for those with the best or the worst of intentions, a fa-vourite with strollers, loungers, and all types of tradesmen — booksel-lers, toothpullers, jugglers — and pick-pockets. 314 very varied mascarons decorated the twelve spans. Until 1813, a pump used to supply the water for the Louvre. A carving on it represented the woman from Samaria pouring water for Christ hence the name of the large store in the rue de la Monnaie, the « Samaritaine »). In the 19th centu-ry, Baltard designed the lamphol-ders which can Still be seen today.

Restoration has taken place on several occasions, but without da-maging the structure of the base of the bridge.

THE SAINTE-CHAPELLE
(Cité metro station)

It was St. Louis who, in 1246 commissioned the building of this gem of Gothic architecture which was completed in less than three years. The architect is thought to have been Pierre de Montreuil. The king wanted a church worthy to house the relics of the Holy Cross and the Crown of Thorns bought from the last French emperor of Constantinople. Originally the chapel was connected to the King's apartments only by a gallery. Today it is an integral part of the vast complex surrounding the Law Courts. Only its tall steeple, which has been rebuilt on more than one occasion, stands out from the rest, 240 ft. above the ground.

Like all the private chapels of the day, it was a two-storey construction. The upper level was reserved for the nobility; the lower chapel for palace staff and people from outside.

The **Lower Chapel**, dedicated to the Virgin Mary, is only 23 ft high. It has three aisles. The original decoration, a blend of colonnettes and three-lobed arcading, was highlighted in the 19th century by the excessive use of polychrome colouring.

The **Upper Chapel** is suffused with a majestic light from its stained glass windows that are 49 ft. high and 13 ft. wide, replacing the walls and subtly lightening the architecture.

The Upper Chapel.

The Sainte-Chapelle (opposite).

The Lower Chapel (pages 102-103).

More than half the **stained glass** is original, the rest having been restored in the 19th century. The windows cover almost 6,500 feet and contain some 1,000 illustrations. Each window deals with one particular subject. The drawings are based on the Old Testament, the story of the relics, Christ's Passion and the life of St. John the Baptist. The great **rose window** in the front, which was rebuilt in the late 15th-century, illustrates the story of the Apocalypse. The single aisle is 65 ft. high and 55 ft. wide. The relics of the Passion used to be on view behind the altar, beneath the gilded wooden canopy. Of the two wooden staircases, only the one on the left is original. The Sainte-Chapelle, which was damaged by fire in 1630 and later ransacked, was rebuilt in the last century under the guidance of Viollet-le-Duc.

SAINT-ÉTIENNE-DU-MONT
(Luxembourg R.E.R. station or Cardinal-Lemoine metro station)

In the 13th century on the mountain named after St. Genevieve, there was an abbey whose church soon proved to be too small for the ever-increasing population that followed the founding of the various university colleges. In 1220, building work started on a new church dedicated to St. Stephen and it too was extended, in 1492. The work, though, was very slow-going and was not completed until 1626.

This is why the church bears traces of successive architectural styles. The façade which was built rather late (in the early 17th century) is a blend of Gothic and Renaissance architecture. The chancel and nave are Flamboyant

The Church of Saint-Etienne-du-Mont (above).

Holding a golden sceptre, the Angel of the Abyss rides a horse with a man's head, pursued by a plague of locusts (Apocalypse IX, v.11) (page 104).

The roodscreen in Saint-Etienne-du-Mont (overleaf).

Gothic. The lower section of the tower dates from 1492 but was the last part of the church to be completed. The outstanding unusual feature of the church is its **roodscreen** (the only one left in Paris) which was built between 1521 and 1545. It was probably Philibert Delorme who designed this Flamboyant Gothic gallery separating the nave and the chancel. The side doors, added in the very early years of the 17th-century, are Classical in style. The pulpit was partly the work of Germain Pilon in 1651, and the organ was built by Jean Buron in the 17th century (although it has been restored on several occasions since then).

The Church of Saint-Eustache.

Saint-Étienne-du-Mont (literally « St. Stephen's on the Hill ») also has some very fine 16th and 17th-century **stained glass windows** (including the original windows in the « ossuary » cloisters), a number of canvases, and epitaphs to Racine and Pascal who were buried here. It houses the relics of St. Genevieve, in a gilded brass reliquary dating from the 19th-century.

SAINT-EUSTACHE
(Les Halles metro station)

Built on the site of a chapel dedicated in the 13th century to St. Agnes, the church now bears the name of St. Eustache, a Roman soldier who was converted to Catholicism then martyred in the 2nd Century. The building work, which began in **1532**, lasted for more than a century, making it a Renaissance church over Gothic foundations. In size, it is similar to Notre-Dame — 340 ft. long and 140 ft. wide with arches 107

grammarian Vaugelas, the composer Rameau, Admiral de Tourville, La Fontaine, Mirabeau and Molière were all buried here.

Saint-Eustache is also the **musicians' church**. Berlioz first presented his « Te Deum » here, and Liszt played his « Gran Mass » in the church. The great organ, with its 85 stops and 7,000 pipes, is now used for numerous concerts.

The church was damaged by fire in 1844 and restored by Baltard.

SAINT-GERMAIN-DES-PRÉS
(Saint-Germain-des-Prés metro station)

The history of the conventual church of Saint-Germain-des-Prés is closely linked to that of the successive abbeys which stood on the site over the centuries, in a series of demolitions and reconstructions inflicted on this very ancient building. In the 6th century, St. Germain, Bishop of Paris, and Clovis' son, Childebert, decided to build a church to house St. Vincent's tunic which had been brought back from Spain. Both of them were, in fact, to be buried in the chapel which took the name Saint-Germain (« les Prés » being a reference to the nearby Clerks' Fields). In the 8th century, the monks adopted the Rule of St. Benedict whose order had become particularly popular on this bank of the Seine. The abbey withstood attack by Norman invaders four times in 40 years. It was rebuilt c. 1000 A.D. (the present church dates from this period) in the purest of Romanesque styles which can still be picked out in certain parts that have remained almost intact. Pope Alexander III consecrated the chancel in the 12th century (at the same time as Notre-Dame). The

ft. high. The pillars in the nave belong to the three ancient orders of architecture — Ionic, Doric and Corinthian. The very fine stained glass windows in the apse date from the 17th century. St. Eustache is shown in the centre, surrounded by the Fathers of the Church and the Apostles. The chapels are decorated with frescoes and statues ("Colbert and Plenitude" by Coysevox, "Fidelity" by Tuby and the Virgin Mary by Pigalle). The church has been the setting for many major events in Parisian life — the christenings of Molière, Mme de Pompadour et Richelieu, Louis XIV 's first communion, and Lulli's wedding. Colbert, the poet Voiture, the

Saint-Germain-des-Prés.

century. It concerned the final storey of the belltower, the steeple and the interior decoration (the frescoes are by Flandrin, one of Ingres' pupils). The church contains the tombs of the de Castellan brothers by Girardon, of Jean Casimir King of Poland (17th century) by the Marsy brothers, and of Descartes, Boileau, and the scientists Mabillon and Montfaucon.

SAINT-GERMAIN-L'AUXERROIS
(Louvre metro station)

Opposite the Louvre colonnade a Neogothic belfry separates the town hall of the First Ward, built in the 19th-century in the Renaissance style, from this most composite of churches. Built on the site of an 8th-century sanctuary, it was dedicated to St. Germain, Bishop of Auxerre. Building work lasted from the 12th to the 15th century, with wide-ranging alterations in the 18th century and a disastrous restoration project in the 19th.

In the 14th century, it was the **chapel of the Kings of France** who lived in the Louvre. It was from its Romanesque tower that the fatal peal of bells heralded the St. Bartholomew's Day massacre on the night of 24th August 1572. The church, though, was also the setting for the wedding of Molière and Armande Béjart. Many of the artists from the Louvre were buried there — the poets Jodelle and Malherbe, the painters Boucher and Coypel, the architects Le Vau, Le Mercier and Soufflot, and the sculptors Coysevox and Coustou.

The Flamboyant Gothic porch was the work of Jean Gaussel in the 15th century. The central doorway dates from the 13th cen-

doorway dates from this same century but the porch was built in 1607. In the 13th century, Pierre de Montreuil, the architect behind the Sainte-Chapelle, built the Gothic cloisters, refectory and dorter. In 1631, the Rule of St. Maur replaced that of St. Benedict. With

the Revolution came the setting up of a saltpeter factory in the ransacked church; the two transept towers were demolished and the carved capitals in the nave were transferred to the Cluny Museum.

A final wave of restoration, under Baltard, arrived in the l7th

111

The Church of Saint-Germain-l'Auxerrois (opposite, left).

The organ in Saint-Germain-l'Auxerrois (opposite, right).

...ury. The transept, nave, side ...isles and polychrome statues of ...t. Vincent and St. Germain are ...ll 15th century.

Some very fine works of art ...ave been preserved unharmed ...e.g. the 17th-century **pew** prob-...bly reserved for the royal family, the 16th-century **carved wooden tryptic**, and the 15th century **Flemish reredos**. In the 18th century, however, the canons decided to modernise the church (demolishing the Renaissance roodscreen made by Lescot and Goujon, the fluting round the pillars in the chancel, and the carvings on the capitals, and replacing the 14th-century stained glass by opaque glass). Ransacked during the Revolution, the church was rather unskilfully restored (especially in the chancel) by Lassus and Baltard in 1855.

The statue of Henri IV.

The church in the Sorbonne.

THE SORBONNE
(Cluny-Sorbonne metro station)

In 1253, in the wake of the new University that had finally shaken off the hold of the episcopacy, St. Louis' chaplain Robert le Sorbon founded a **theological college** for sixteen poor students. The « Sorbonne » quickly gained real power (or counterbalancing power) which was to be of great importance during the Ancien Régime. In the 13th century, it protested against the Order of the Knights Templar. It condemned Joan of Arc in 1431 and gave its support to the Leaguers against the Protestants in the 16th century. In 1626 Richelieu, its then rector, had the Sorbonne rebuilt and extended by Le Mercier who also built a Jesuit-style **church**. Today it houses the **Cardinal's tomb** made entirely of white marble and carved by Girardon in 1694 according to drawings by Le Brun.

There was a second rebuilding project in the late 19th century under the leadership of the architect Nénot. It left the church untouched and it can still be seen today in its original state.

The Sorbonne is now the centre of Paris University III and IV.

THE STATUE OF HENRI IV
(Pont-Neuf metro station)

In 1818, a new statue of Henri IV (nicknamed the « gay old spark » or « Vert-Galant ») was erected in place of the one sculpted by John of Bologna which had been destroyed in 1792. It was François-Frédéric Lemot who cast the monument, using bronze from statues of Napoleon since he had fallen from favour by that time. A flight of steps behind the statue leads to the small Vert-Galant **Gardens** from which there is a view across the quays to the Mint and the Louvre.

THE EIFFEL TOWER
(Bir-Hakeim Metro station)
(Champ-de-Mars station on the R.E.R.)

Built in the late 19th century, the Eiffel Tower was an act of defiance on the part of an engineer vis-à-vis traditional forms of architecture. It was a wager as regards building materials for it made use of all the possibilities afforded by glass and steel, and as regards its size. With a height of almost 1,000 feet, it towered far above the Panthéon which, at 257 feet, was at that time the tallest building in Paris. In fact, the tower remained the tallest building in the world for many years. Its design, too, was new—it stands on concrete foundations but the keyword for the three storeys was lightness. Its weight, 700 metric tonnes, is less than the weight of the mass of air it cuts through. Even the strongest winds cannot move the tip more than 5 ins., and heat causes a maximum dilation of 6 ins.

Seven hundred projects were submitted, all of them concerning « the possibility of erecting an iron tower with a 406 ft. square

The gardens of the Champ-de-Mars seen from the Eiffel Tower.

116

base and a height of almost 1,000 ft. » It was Gustave Eiffel's plans which won the day. He had already worked on the construction of viaducts and built the railway bridge across the R. Garonne in Bordeaux. For the **1889 World Fair** in Paris, he succeeded in doing something that had already failed in Turin and Philadelphia. The building work took 2 years and 3 months. Three hundred workmen assembled the 15,000 pieces of metal containing 7 million holes using 2,500,000 rivets.

Now an accepted part of the Paris skyline, the tower undergoes regular maintenance. Every 7 years, workmen spend a total of 20,000 hours covering it with the 50 tonnes of paint that it absorbs, in honour of the three million or so visitors who come to admire it every year. They can, if they wish, climb the 1,710 steps stopping, of course, at each floor. On the first platform (185 ft. above ground level) is an **audiovisual museum** retracing the tower's history. A restaurant welcomes visitors to the second floor 374 ft. up. And, in exceptionally fine weather, the wonderful view from the third floor (891 ft. above the ground) stretches over more than 43 miles. The glass-walled gallery has a bar and a restaurant, a souvenir shop and a post office. It was on this floor that Eiffel had his « flat. » Beneath the legs of the towers is a bust sculpted by Bourdelle paying homage to the audacity of the engineer, a man who created this ingenious trophy of an industrial civilisation that was then in its heyday. The Eiffel Tower has, in fact, been praised in poems by Apollinaire, Cocteau and Aragon, and in paintings by Pissaro, Dufy and Utrillo, before it was reduced to miniature size and reproduced to excess. It has also been involved in the deve-

The Eiffel Tower.

lopment of new **communication** techniques. In 1892, it was used in a radioelectric link-up with the Panthéon. In 1908, it acquired a military radio station which made use of the possibilities then afforded by the techniques of wireless, and in 1918 it became the head office of French Broadcasting. The television mast installed in 1957 has brought the tower's overall height up to **1,042 ft.** And since 1947, it has had lights on it for aviation.

The tower dominates the vast stretch of grass that is the **Champ-de-Mars**, laid out according to plans drawn by Gabriel in 1765 and originally used as an exercise ground for the Military

Academy (hence its name). Before the Revolution, it was used for the first experiments with hot-air balloons and for the first horse races. In 1790, it was the setting for the Festival of the Federation during which 300,000 federates swore an oath to the newly-constituted nation. In 1794, Robespierre who had created a State religion led a ceremony in honour of the Supreme Being here. The Champ-de-Mars later became a showground, and the site of the World Fairs. In 1928, Formigé finished laying out the gardens half-a-mile long and 270 yds. wide bordered by luxury housing.

TOUR SAINT-JACQUES
St. James' Tower
(Châtelet metro station)

This is all that remains of St. James' Church, which was built during the reign of François I and demolished in 1797 by its purchaser (it had been auctioned off) who had nevertheless promised to preserve the belltower. It is 170 ft. high, 32 ft. wide at the top, and 42 ft. wide at its base. Built in the Flamboyant Gothic style, extensive restoration was carried out by Ballu in 1859 and it was reinforced by a bank of earth when the rue de Rivoli was laid out. It is decorated with a number of statues, including one of Pascal who carried out physics experiments here and another of St. James the Elder (sculpted by Chenillon in 1870). In 1871, a met. station was set up at the top of the tower.

St. James' Tower.

La Villette.

THE VAL-DE-GRACE
(Saint-Jacques metro station)

In 1624 Anne of Austria, wife of Louis XIII, brought the Benedictine nuns from Val-Profond (which then lay outside the Paris boundary) to this abbey in the rue Saint-Jacques. She had an apartment furnished for her own use, a place she came to for rest away from the intrigues of the Louvre, but more especially a place in which to pray for the birth of an heir. When her wish was fulfilled, she had a magnificent **church** built in thanks — her son, Louis XIV, laid the foundation stone in **1645**. Mansart, and later Lemercier and Le Muet, designed the Baroque building whose tall dome is of Italian inspiration. Inside, the cupola is decorated with a fresco by Mignard representing « The Dwelling Place of the Blessed ». Anguier carved the bas-reliefs in the chapels. The High Altar with its gigantic baldaquin decorated with rope-moulding was designed by Le Duc and is reminiscent of the one in St. Peter's in Rome. The St. Louis Chapel leads into the arched galleries of the cloisters. The convent was turned into a **military hospital** during the Revolution and has retained this function up to the present day. By doing so, it was able to escape being ransacked and to keep its original buildings. One of the galleries in the cloisters houses a **Health Service Museum**.

121

LA VILLETTE
(Porte-de-la-Villette or Porte-de-Pantin metro station)

The former site of the cattle market and slaughterhouses (136 acres) has been given over to a gigantic urban development project. From the Porte de Pantin to the south to the Porte de la Villette to the north, the **park**, cut in two by the Ourcq Canal, has brought back traditions dating from the 17th and 18th centuries when gardens were places in which to meet and enjoy activities that were a blend of urbanity, pleasure and experiment. The park now includes several attractions e.g. shows, restaurants, play areas and cultural centres, all set out in the midst of the lawns, paths and gardens, and all of them centring on six major sites - the Villette Centre, the Science and Industry Centre, the Geode, the Zenith Concert Hall, the Grand Hall, and the Music Centre.

It was **Bernard Tschumi** who, in 1983, was commissioned to landscape the 86 acres of urban parkland (listed as a "public building"). He balanced the open spaces around three unusual systems:

- **the buildings (follies)**. Laid out to a regular pattern every 390 ft. they bring scale and points of interest to the park. The "cubes", with sides measuring 35 ft, are covered with bright red enamelled iron. They are both sculptures and activity centres. Each Folly has a specific purpose (an external slide for the children's Folly, a weathervane for the La Ville café etc.).

- **the two galleries** set at right angles to each other link the two gates (the Villette Gallery with its corrugated canopy) or run along the canal (Ourcq Gallery, a light transparent construction). The shrub-lined **promenade**, on the other hand, winds its way through the park.

- **the open spaces** bring a breath of fresh air into the park. The two geometrically-shaped lawns covering an area of almost 20 acres are popular with those out for a stroll, with concert audiences and with anybody who enjoys outdoor games.

The **gardens** were designed partly by Alexandre Clementoff (the "Energy Garden" which lies 20 ft. below the level of the remainder of the park and which shows bamboo off in all its splendour) and partly by Gilles Vexlard who designed a "terraced" garden and planted a vine in it.

The furniture was designed by **Philippe Starck**. Famous designers such as Daniel Buren or Jean Nouvel also contributed to the architecture and layout.

The park will not be finished until 1991, when the galleries and gardens will be completed, the restaurants will have been built, and a glasshouse, pony club, aquatic centre, video centre and children's play area will all be ready for use.

On the north and south sides, there will be two property developments including housing, offices, shops and a hotel.

The **Villette House** (1867) to the north, which is also known as the "vets' rotunda" tells the everyday story of the district and neighbourhoods nearby. The mezzanine is a permanent exhibition centre telling the tale of one hundred years in the life of the slaughterhouses. The ground floor is used for temporary exhibitions etc.

The building stands on the esplanade of the **Science and Industry Centre** that was opened in 1986. Adrien Fainsilber, the

winner of the competition first launched in 1980, designed the interior layout of the building (877 ft. long, 357 ft. wide and 130,00 ft. high), basing it on the triple theme of water, plant life, and natural light, " the source of energy for the living world".

The centre is designed to be "interactive", a place in which man can meet up with sciences and techniques at his own speed.

The Geode in the Villette Park.

Explora, the permanent exhibition housed in an area of 322,800 sq. ft., is laid out around four main centres of human activity i.e. "From earth to universe", "The adventure of life", "Matter and human labour", and "Languages and communication".

Two other areas (7,532 and 26,900 sq. ft.) are used for temporary exhibitions.

The 275-seat **planetarium** brings to life current events from the world of astronomy and astrophysics.

The **inventorium** is reserved for children.

The Centre also has a media library, a science-current events room, an international conference centre, a cinema ("Louis-Lumière"), a training centre and a research centre. It can also cater

for school parties undertaking "Villette study trips".

The **Geode** (1985), which was also designed by Fainsilber, is the only one of its kind in the world. It is a sphere 117 ft. in diameter covered in polished stainless steel. The auditorium contains 370 "wrap-around" seats. The hemispherical screen (with a surface of 10,760 sq. ft.) produces very pure sound thanks

123

to the inclusion of tiny perforated aluminium sheets. The sound is spread throughout the auditorium by twelve loudspeakers set up behind the screen, which increases the feeling of depth of vision. Both the auditorium and the screen slope at an angle of 30°.

Opened in January 1984, the **Zenith** is used exclusively for variety shows and rock concerts and can seat up to 6,000 people. It provides a maximum of comfort and security and has the best possible acoustics.

The **Great Hall**, once the cattle market (1867), is a metallic structure that has been used since 1985 for concerts, festivals, shows and various exhibitions. It is 783 ft. long, 279 ft. wide and 61 ft. high and can cater for 15,900 people. It has a modular style of architecture - the main hall, for example, can be divided into two sections. The basement contains the Boris Vian Room (300 seats).

The **Paris-Villette Theatre**, which was founded in 1972 under the name "Théâtre Présent" in the former Exchange Pavilion, is a place of expression for contemporary authors.

Finally, the **Music Centre** project was commissioned from Christian de Portzamparc. It will eventually house the National Academy of Music, now in the Rue de Madrid, a 1200-seat concert hall, the Inter-Contemporary Centre whose president is Pierre Boulez, a Museum of Instruments, the Institute for Music Teaching and Choreography (set up in 1984), study rooms, a media library, and accommodation as well as schooling for music students.

The aim is to abolish the segregation that exists at present between the different musical disciplines and to bring together repertoires, courses, creation and reseach, with teaching and conservation.

On the Pont des Arts.

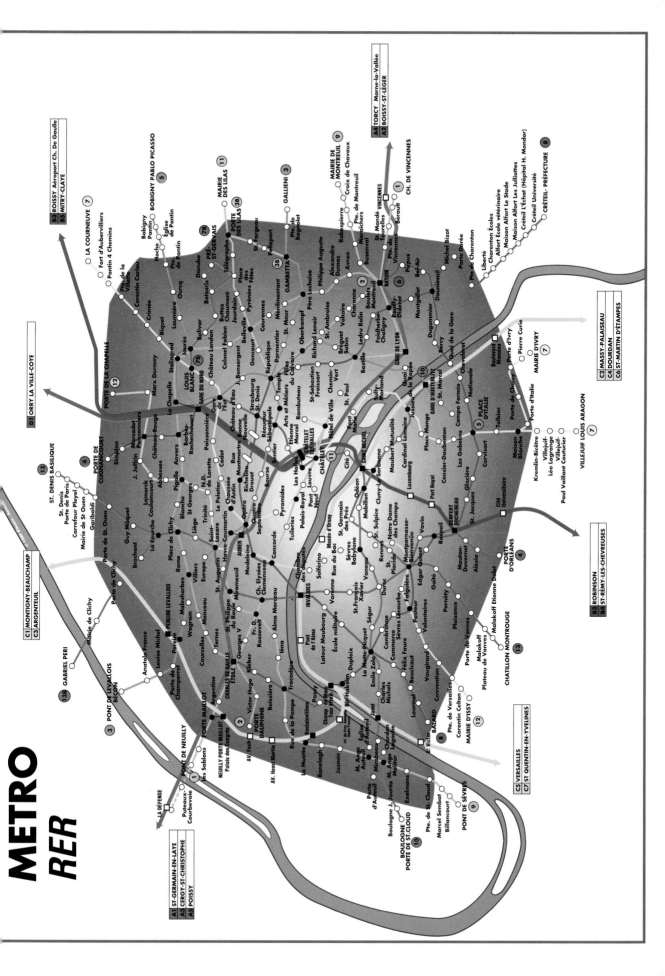

METRO
RER

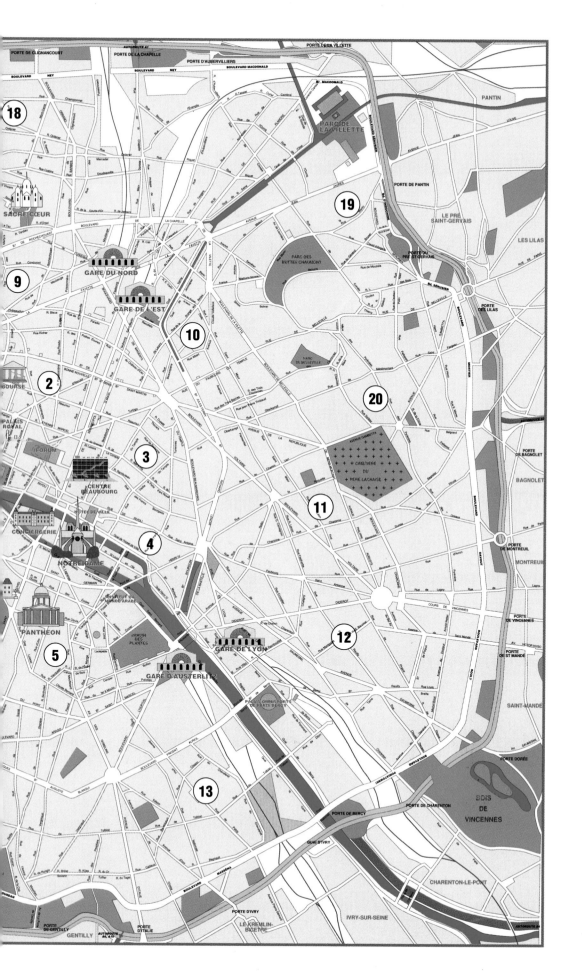

TABLE OF CONTENTS

Introduction 3

Arc de Triomphe...9

Arche de la Défense.......................................11

Bastille...13

Beaubourg 14

National Library 15

Champs-Elysées 19

Comédie Française 19

Conciergerie 22

Concorde (place de la)..................................24

Military Academy...26

Grand Palais and Petit Palais.......................27

Cluny Residence 29

Mint 31

City Hall 32

Ile Saint-Louis 36

Institut de France 36

Institut du Monde Arabe...............................37

Invalides 38

Louvre 43

Madeleine Church 56

Marais District 56

Ministry of Finance 60

Montmartre 61

Orsay Art Gallery 66

Notre-Dame 69

Observatory 79

Opera House 79

Bastille Opera House 82

Palais de Chaillot..83

Law Courts 86

Palais du Luxembourg..................................87

Palais-Royal..90

Panthéon 92

Place des Victoires..95

Place Vendôme 96

Pont-Neuf 97

Sainte-Chapelle...100

Sainte-Etienne-du-Mont (church).................105

Saint-Eustache (church)................................108

Sainte-Germain-des-Prés 109

Saint-Germain-l'Auxerrois (church) 111

Sorbonne...115

Statue of Henri IV...116

Eiffel Tower 116

St. James' Tower 120

Val-de-Grâce 121

Villette..122

PHOTOGRAPHIC CREDITS

All the photos in this book were by **Hervé Boulé** except the following :

Hervé Champollion : pages 15, 16-17, 19, 20-21, 29, 40h, 57, 58, 62, 72-73, 118.

Michel Dillange : pages 18, 23.

Nicolas Fediaevsky : pages 100, 102, 103, 104.

Jean-Paul Gisserot : pages 31, 34-35, 40b, 41, 49, 50-51, 71, 80-81, 86, 88-89, 98-99, 101, 120.

Philippe Thomas : pages 74, 75, 77.

Yves Violette : pages 30, 78, 84, 85.

My grateful thanks to Hélène Amato-D.-P. for her valuable assistance.

Cet ouvrage a été imprimé par Mame Tours (37)
I.S.B.N. 2.7373.0565.9 - Dépôt légal : mai 1990
N° éditeur : 1865.02.09.02.91